75 Easy Earth Science Demonstrations

Thomas Kardos

illustrated by Nicholas Soloway

J. WESTON WALCH
PUBLISHER
PORTLAND, MAINE

Dedication

This book is dedicated to my darling wife, Pearl, who throughout this project assisted me with great patience. As a nonscience educator, she helped me develop this book into an easy-to-use and comprehensible resource.

Cover photo: Agate

1   2   3   4   5   6   7   8   9   10

ISBN 0-8251-2907-9

Copyright © 1997
J. Weston Walch, Publisher
P.O. Box 658 • Portland, Maine 04104-0658

Printed in the United States of America

Contents

Preface

As a middle school teacher, many times I found myself wishing for a quick and easy demonstration to illustrate a word, a concept, or a principle in science. Also, I wanted a brief explanation to conveniently review basics and additional facts without looking through many texts.

This book is a collection of many classroom demonstrations. Explanation is provided so that you can quickly review key concepts. Basic scientific ideas are hard to present on a concrete level; this book fills that specific need. Some of the demonstrations can be repeated at home and also can be adapted by you as student laboratory activities. A few require more time than just one class period.

The actual teacher demonstration is something full of joy and expectation, like a thriller with an unexpected twist ending. Keep it that way and enjoy it! Try everything beforehand.

We need to support each other by leaving footprints in the sands of time. Teaching is a living art. Happy journey! Happy sciencing!

—*Thomas Kardos*

Introduction

My Philosophy of Education

My personal philosophy of education involves many themes:

1. Students must feel like participants in the joy of science.

2. Students need many hands-on experiences. Invite them to experiment at home. This invitation must be limited by the availability of equipment and the relative safety of the activity. Many experiments can be done with informal equipment such as recycled jars, soda cans, and bottles. Inexpensive plastic measuring cups can replace graduated cylinders.

3. Students need to form in their own minds a concept of what science is. Do not encourage rote memorization. Science is a series of stories that need the participant's intervention. Let your students jump in and get involved in these stories.

4. Teachers do not have to answer all student questions. It is wonderful to let your students know that you are a limited resource. Let students go out and find answers to some difficult questions. Maybe there are no answers. Nobody on this planet has all the answers. It is important that you teach your students the concept that humans have limits, but these can change. Let students know that through networking (cooperative effort) they, too, can find some of the harder answers.

5. People are concrete operators. Their learning starts with real objects and lots of manipulations and eventually ends in abstract reasoning and concept formation. This is why people draw sketches for you, to explain their ideas. Read summaries or explanations of Piaget's learning theory; it will change your teaching style for life.

6. Be open to change. Be prepared to change as you progress in teaching. The world around us changes and so must our teaching style.

7. Finally, realize that you cannot do it all. Your many science students become your followers. You will start a science revolution! This is your real opportunity!

Suggestions for Teachers

1. A • (bullet) denotes a demonstration. Several headings have multiple demonstrations.

2. MATERIALS: Provides an accurate list of materials needed. You can make substitutions and changes, as you find appropriate.

3. Since many demonstrations are small and are not clearly visible from the back of the room, you will need to take this into account as part of your classroom-management technique. Students need to see the entire procedure, step by step.

4. Some demonstrations require that students make observations over a short period of time. It is important that they observe the changes in progress. One choice is to videotape the event and replay it several times.

5. Some demonstrations can be enhanced by bottom illumination: Place the demonstration on the overhead projector and lower the mirror so that no image is projected overhead.

6. Encourage students to repeat certain carefully selected demonstrations in class or at home.

7. Key words are included in the Index for easier access to the demonstrations.

8. I use a 30-cup coffeepot to heat water for student experiments and to perform many demonstrations in lieu of an electric hot plate, pans, and more cumbersome equipment.

9. I may use temperature Fahrenheit in some places, since most younger students relate to it better.

10. A few demonstrations may appear difficult to set up, for they have many parts. Be patient, follow the listing's steps, and you will really succeed with them.

Equipment

• Sometimes, though rarely, I will call for equipment that you may not have. An increasing growth in technology tends to complicate matters. Skip these few demonstrations or borrow the equipment from your local high school teacher. Review with him or her the proper and safe use of the equipment. These special demonstrations will add immensely to your power as an effective educator and will enhance your professionalism.

- Try all demonstrations in advance to smooth your show. If something fails, enjoy it and teach with it. Many great science discoveries had to be done over many times before their first success. Dr. Land had to do more than 11,000 experiments to develop the instant color photograph. Most people would have quit long before that.

- One of my favorite techniques is to use a camcorder and show the demonstration on a large monitor.

Disclaimer

The safety rules are provided only as a guide. They are neither complete nor totally inclusive. The publisher and the author do not assume any responsibility for actions or consequences in following instructions provided in this demonstration book.

SAFETY PROCEDURES

- Follow all local, state, and federal safety procedures: Protect your students and yourself from harm.

- Attend safety classes to be up-to-date on the latest in classroom safety procedures. Much new legislation has been adopted in the recent past.

- Have evacuation plans clearly posted, planned, and actually tested.

- Have an ABC-rated fire extinguisher on hand at all times. Use a Halon™ gas extinguisher for electronic equipment.

- Learn how to use a fire extinguisher properly.

- Label all containers and use original containers.

- Wear required safety equipment when handling hazardous materials, such as laboratory acids or anything stronger than ordinary vinegar.

- Practice your demonstration if it is totally new to you. A few demonstrations do require some prior practice.

- Conduct demonstrations at a distance so that no one is harmed, should anything go wrong.

- Have students wash their hands whenever they come into contact with anything that may be remotely harmful to them—even if years later—like lead.

- Neutralize all acids and bases prior to disposal.

- Dispose of demonstration materials in a safe way. Obtain your district's guidelines on this matter.

1. INSIDE THE EARTH

If one looked at the earth in cross section one would observe the **crust**, the **mantle**, the **outer core**, and the **inner core**.

MATERIALS: hard-boiled egg, knife

- Cut a hard-boiled egg and show the students the cross section. The egg has three layers: the shell, the white, and the yolk. Similarly, a cross section of the earth would reveal that it is structured in layers.

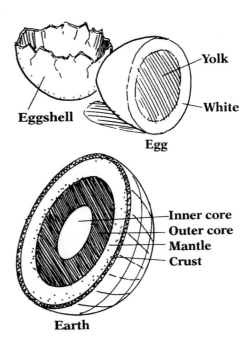

2. CORE SAMPLES

When geologists need information about the earth's structure, they drill for **core samples**.

MATERIALS: straw, cupcake with filling and icing, razor blade, camcorders and monitor (optional)

- Gently insert the straw down through the middle of the cupcake. Remove the straw and carefully cut it open to observe the "core sample" of icing, cake, and filling. Use a camcorder, if available, to show a close-up of the entire demonstration.

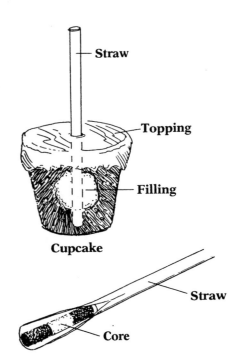

3. HARDNESS TEST: MOHS SCALE

The hardness test is critical in determining the properties of minerals. Follow the instructions of your hardness test kit. Use the close-up features of a camcorder, if one is available. The hardness scale is provided for your convenience.

MOHS HARDNESS SCALE

HARDNESS SCALE 1–10 SAMPLE MATERIALS	TEST FOR HARDNESS
1. Talcum	Softest of materials; can be scratched by anything, even fingernail
2. Gypsum	Can be scratched by anything except talcum
3. Calcite	Can be scratched by a copper wire or penny
4. Fluorite	Can be scratched by steel tool, knife, or nail file, but not easily
5. Apatite	Can be scratched by steel tool or nail file, but not easily
6. Feldspar	Can scratch glass and cannot be scratched by a knife
7. Quartz	Can scratch steel and glass
8. Topaz	Scratches quartz
9. Corundum	Scratches topaz
10. Diamond	Can scratch everything else

There is also a hardness scale 1–15. The diamond is also the hardest mineral on that scale.

MATERIALS: hardness testing kit, sample minerals and materials, camcorder and monitor (optional), diamond-tipped glass cutter, small pieces of glass

- Test the hardness of several rocks, minerals, and other materials, using the hardness test kit.

- Scratch several lines on a piece of glass with the diamond-tipped cutter.

4. STREAK TEST FOR MINERALS

MATERIALS: several minerals (whatever minerals you may have), ceramic tile (preferably with light-colored back)

- **Streaking** is an excellent test for identifying minerals. When you write on your chalkboard, you are streaking your chalk, or calcite, on the chalkboard surface. Minerals leave a characteristic powdery trail, called a streak. Some minerals seem to have several colors, but when you streak them, they leave a uniform color. Using several minerals, demonstrate streaking on the porous back of a ceramic tile.

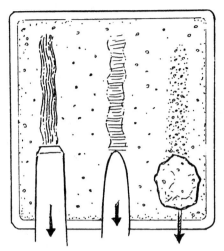

Back of ceramic tile

5. TESTING MINERALS FOR MAGNETISM

Minerals that contain iron and cobalt have **magnetic** properties.

MATERIALS: magnet, minerals, compass

- Test the minerals with the magnet to see if they are attracted by it. Lodestone or other minerals containing large percentages of iron will be attracted, as will some meteorites.

- Place the compass near the mineral to be tested to see if the needle moves. If it does, the material is magnetic.

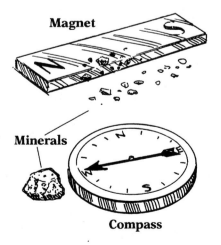

Magnet

Minerals

Compass

6. TESTING MINERALS FOR CALCITE

Calcite is a soft, ususally clear or white mineral. It is a base, and it reacts with acids by fizzing.

MATERIALS: calcite mineral, weak hydrochloric acid (.5M solution), eyedropper

CAUTION! Wear apron, gloves, and goggles when mixing the acid. For the experiment with calcite, use gloves, glasses, and an apron.

- Place several drops of weak hydrochloric acid on a rock suspected of being calcite. If it fizzes, it is calcite. Calcite is the only mineral to fizz with an acid.

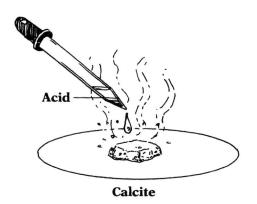

7. OBSERVING CRYSTAL SHAPES OF MINERALS

Minerals with a definite shape of their own are crystals. One thinks immediately of diamonds and other precious stones as cut crystals.

MATERIALS: sand, sugar, salt, several minerals with visible crystalline shape, magnifying glass

- Using the magnifying glass, look at sand, sugar, salt, and mineral samples to observe their specific crystalline shapes.

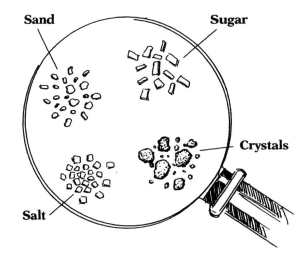

8. VARYING THE SIZE OF CRYSTALS

When igneous rocks cool slowly, they have larger crystals. Sometimes igneous rocks have such small crystals that they are called texture. Texture is used to identify different igneous rocks like granite, rhyolite, quartz, feldspar, and mica.

MATERIALS: two crucibles, beaker, water, teaspoon, sulfur powder, forceps, Bunsen burner, magnifying glass

- Place a teaspoon of powdered sulfur in one of the crucibles. Allow it to melt and then cool slowly. Place a teaspoon of powdered sulfur in the second crucible. Half-fill the beaker with water. Melt the sulfur and pour it slowly into the beaker. Students will notice that the sulfur that cooled slowly developed larger crystals than the sulfur that cooled rapidly in water.

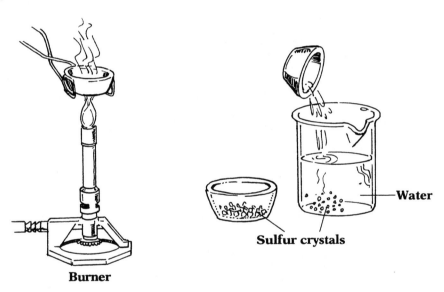

Burner

Sulfur crystals

Water

9. FORMATION OF SEDIMENTARY ROCKS

MATERIALS: jar, soil, sand, pebbles, gravel, water, teaspoon, paper cup

- Place a mix of sand, pebbles, and soil in a jar about half-full of water. Stir vigorously and let the mixture stand for a while. Students will notice that the heavier materials settle to the bottom. They are the **sediments**. The materials that settle on the top are smaller and lighter. They are the **particles**.

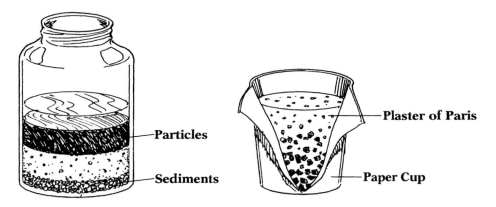

- Mix some pebbles and gravel with some plaster of Paris. Fill the paper cup with the mixture and let it harden. Peel away the paper cup and observe the sedimentary rock.

10. FORMING SEDIMENTARY ROCKS BY EVAPORATION #1

MATERIALS: salt, beaker, tablespoon, water, evaporation dish, hot plate

- Half-fill the beaker with water and dissolve several tablespoons of salt. Heat the dish until all the water evaporates. What is left behind is a sedimentary rock: **halite**. Limestone and halite are examples of sedimentary rocks formed by evaporation. Limestone contains calcite.

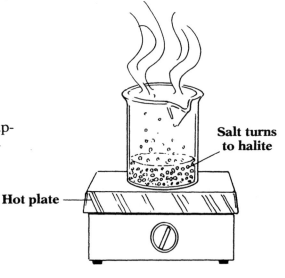

...NG SEDIMENTARY ROCKS BY
...VAPORATION #2

...ve icicle-like formations hanging from the ceiling ...**talactites** hang down, while **stalagmites** project ...in and become solid columns. These sedimentary .... They were formed by the dripping and evaporating ...ry long periods of time.

.... two beakers, water, Epsom salt, cotton string, small dish

- Fill both beakers nearly three-quarters full of water. Dissolve the Epsom salt until the water is saturated (no more salt will dissolve). Place the two glasses several inches apart. Place the string into both glasses, with a small bow in the middle. Below the middle of the string, place a small dish to catch the dripping. In about one day, you will notice your own stalactite and stalagmite.

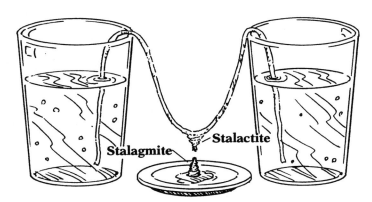

Glasses with water and Epsom salt

12. FORMING SEDIMENTARY ROCKS FROM SHELLS

MATERIALS: coquina (time- and pressure-cemented seashells), seashells, limestone, eyedropper, vinegar

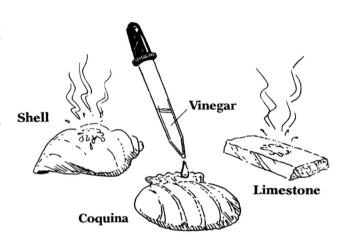

- Place a few drops of vinegar on the shells, **coquina**, or limestone. Notice the bubbles. The calcium carbonate that is part of the shells, coquina, and limestone react with an acid. Calcium carbonate is the same as the mineral calcite.

13. WEATHERING

Nothing remains the same on earth. Changes in water, wind, and temperature break down everything. This breaking down is **weathering**. Moisture fills the small cracks in rocks, freezes, and breaks down the rocks. Plants and trees grow. As their fine roots enter fine cracks in rocks and then grow, the rocks break.

MATERIALS: small plastic bottle with cap, water, freezer

- Fill the bottle with water, cap it, and place it in the freezer. Notice that the water expands as it becomes ice. Water is a powerful weathering factor when combined with temperature.

14. CHEMICAL WEATHER[...]

Another form of weathering is **chemical weathering**. Gases in [...] as carbon dioxide, nitrogen dioxide, and sulfurs, mix with water and fo[...] When it rains, these acids cause the rain to be acid. Acid rain kills trees, po[...] streams and lakes, and dissolves marble, limestone, and other rocks. Airborne acids damage nearly all substances they touch. These airborne pollutants are **photochemical**; they react with the light rays of the sun. The resulting mix is smog. Smog has severe health effects on humans and damages most material objects.

MATERIALS: calcium pill, glass, chicken bone, old tooth, vinegar

- Place the calcium pill in the glass and add some vinegar. Notice the chemical reaction: fizzing, foaming, and the breaking of the pill into smaller bits. Eventually these bits will be neutralized by the acid. This activity closely replicates in fast action the effects of chemical weathering.

- Place a chicken bone or tooth in a beaker and add vinegar. You may substitute any cola drink, for it contains phosphoric acid. Show students how, over a time, the bone or tooth is dissolved by the acid.

Vinegar

Chicken bone

the ground's pores (spaces between its
surface, it becomes groundwater. Water
a layer of clay or rock that is impermeable
rock is porous, it becomes saturated with
water table. Shale, a typical sedimentary
d clay that block water from passing through.
ers of clay, are a natural reservoir to store
for wells. The totality of aquifers in a region

lastic cups or glasses, flask (beaker or glass) with
water.

- Fill the thr... with clay, gravel, and sand. Pour a small amount of
  water into each one. Notice the time it takes for the water to go to the
  bottom. In gravel the action is fairly rapid, in sand it is slower, while in
  clay it may be either very slow or nonexistent. The gravel has the larg-
  est spaces, sand has smaller but sufficient spaces, and clay has such
  fine spaces that if it is compacted it may be impermeable.

Gravel   Sand   Clay   Water

16. SOIL SATURATION

Soil will absorb water until all the spaces between its particles are full. When it cannot absorb any more water, it is **saturated**. In terrain such as the Los Angeles basin, where there is much clay near the surface, saturation can be a problem. During rains, after a brief period of saturation, runoffs may cause flooding.

MATERIALS: beaker, graduated cylinder, sand, water

- Fill a beaker nearly full with sand. Pour water from the graduated cylinder to fill the beaker. The volume of water in the sand represents the voids in sand. Now the sand is saturated. Since sand represents soil, this is an example of saturated soil.

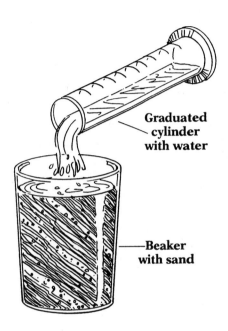

Graduated cylinder with water

Beaker with sand

17. WATER CONSERVATION

Water runoff from mountain springs and rain works its way into lakes, rivers, and eventually oceans. Some of the rainwater percolates (seeps and enters) into the ground, forming aquifers that are tapped for wells. Many cities line their riverbeds with concrete and urban structures, which cover up most of the formerly uncovered soil. Water does not have the opportunity to replenish the dwindling groundwater basin. Most rainfall is lost to runoff.

To save part of the runoff water, the Los Angeles County Flood Control District has established large basins next to rivers, where runoff waters are directed. These spreading basins allow the water to percolate into the aquifers, where it is stored for future use. As a total strategy, water is kept behind dams and slowly released to the spreading basins, unless a storm is announced. Then, by law, the water behind dams must be released to provide storage for the next storm. The purpose of the dams is to slow down the runoff during storms and conserve water.

Gravity or arch dams are usually made from either earth or concrete. Dams do not last indefinitely; they continually develop internal cracks, due to the earth's movement, thermal expansion of the materials, and other stresses. Engineers and engineering geologists continually maintain and inspect dams. All dams must be government certified for safety. Engineers repair dams by drilling core holes into them to find new cracks. Then, using the same holes, they pump in grout, a mix of cement and water to fill internal cracks. Some students may have noticed many capped pipes on the surface structure of dams. Now they know why they are there and what they are used for.

MATERIALS: three large plastic glasses, graduated cylinder, three different soil samples

- Fill three containers nearly full with soil samples, but do not compact them. Saturate each container and measure carefully how much water is needed to fill the glass with soil to the top. This will provide you with data about soil absorption and percolation rates of the soil samples. You can calculate comparative percolation rates by timing water absorption.

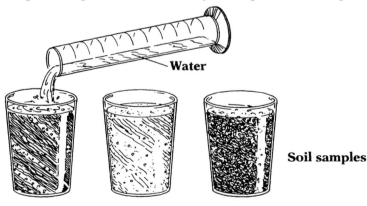

Water

Soil samples

18. SALTWATER INTRUSION INTO AQUIFERS

Coastal cities experience the mixing of seawater with their groundwater basin, making water unusable. To prevent this saltwater intrusion (mixing) into fresh water aquifers, the various water agencies have created a series of wells near the coast. Fresh water is pumped into the wells in large amounts to create a high-pressure barrier. This high-pressure barrier forms a wall that prevents seawater intrusion into the region's groundwater basin. The Los Angeles area has one West Coast Barrier Project in Manhattan Beach and another, the Alamitos Bay Barrier Projects, in the southern region. Additional information is available from the Los Angeles County Flood Control and the United States Coast and Geodetic Service.

MATERIALS: two identical plastic boxes, cup, water, salt, soil

- Fill the boxes three-quarters full of soil. Pour a few cups of tap water into one and a few cups of salt water into the other one. Place the two boxes together. The plastic walls represent the high-pressure wall of the injected water, preventing the two water basins from mixing.

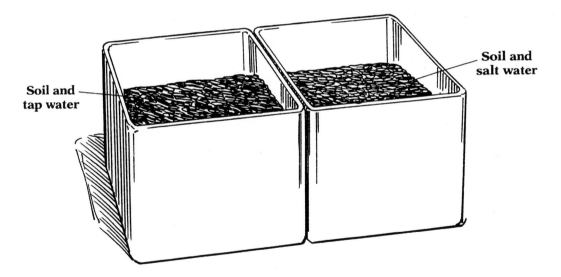

Soil and tap water

Soil and salt water

19. MOTION ACCELERATES EROSION

The motion of water and wind speeds up the long-term effects of **erosion**.

MATERIALS: two identical clean quart jars with covers, water, two pieces of hard candy, measuring cup

- Label one jar as A, the other as B. Put a piece of candy in each jar. Pour two cups of water over each piece of candy. Cover both jars. Place them in a location where they both can be seen. Shake jar A once or twice a day. Do not disturb jar B. Notice the difference after just two days. The disturbed candy has dissolved much more than the undisturbed one. Mud balls dissolve slowly in rain, but when placed near or in a stream of fast-moving water, they dissolve faster. The knocking about by water accelerates erosion.

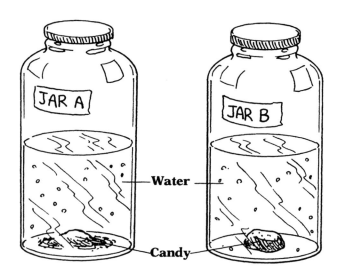

20. FALLING WATER CAUSES EROSION

Rocks beneath waterfalls are slowly eroded by falling water.

MATERIALS: sink with running water, bar of soap, sponge

- Set the bar of soap on the sponge and place it under the faucet. Turn on the faucet and adjust it to a very fine stream. The water must fall on the center of the soap. Let the water run for 30 to 45 minutes and observe. Where the water falls, there will be an indentation. If you let the water run for a much longer time, first a hole would develop and then the entire soap bar would slowly melt away. (To conserve water, this is not necessary.) While rocks are much harder than soap and are not soluble in water, the constant hitting of their surface by water wears them away.

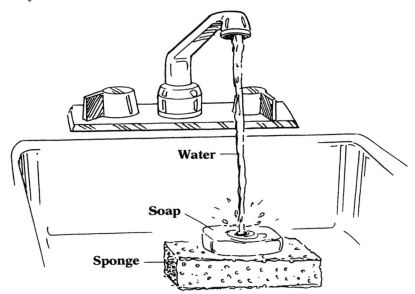

21. MOUNTAINS RISE UP DUE TO EROSION

As the top surfaces of mountains wear away due to erosion, the mountains become lighter and float higher on the earth's mantle. The added weight of erosion sediments causes the seacoast to place additional weight on the mantle. Therefore it slowly sinks. The up-and-down movement of the earth is **isostasy**.

MATERIALS: 2- × 4- × 4-inch wooden block, glass or plastic see-through container at least twice the size of the wood, tablespoon, masking tape, water, marker, plastic sandwich bag, sand

- Place a piece of tape on one side of the wood block, and mark it off in centimeters. Place a piece of tape on one side of the see-through container. Mark it off in centimeters. Half-fill the container with water. Place the block in the water. On top of the block, place the plastic bag with 1 to 2 tablespoons of sand. Mark the level of water on both the container and the block. Carefully remove the plastic bag with the sand. Again observe the level of water on the block and the container. The upward movement of the block models the uplift due to erosion (removal of plastic bag with sand).

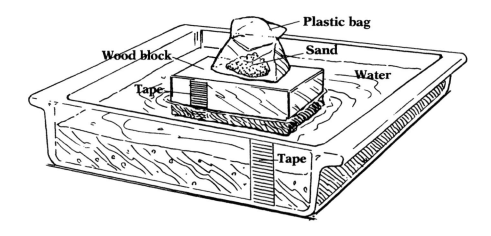

22. GLACIER EROSION

Glaciers are large, deep (one mile or more) rivers of snow on top of ice. Since they are massive, they melt only slightly in the summer near their surface. Glaciers slowly flow down a slope or valley. As they slowly melt and drag along **alluvial** (erosion by-products) materials, they create long ridges of alluvial debris called **moraines**.

MATERIALS: sand, soap, ice cube

- Place the ice cube in the sand. Then scrape the soap with the ice cube. The scratches in the soap represent the scratches made by glaciers. Scratches such as these on the walls and floor of a valley are clues to the presence of ancient glaciers. The bottom glacier ice, while moving, trapped much debris including many rocks. These rocks caused the scratches on the walls and floor of a valley.

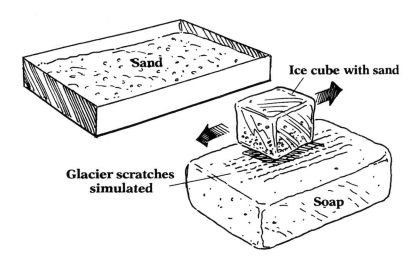

23. WIND EROSION

Wind causes **erosion**—the moving away of the earth's surface materials. If the material is sand, the wind forms **sand dunes** or hills of sand. These dunes have two sides: the **windward** side that faces the wind and the **leeward** side that faces away from the wind. The windward side has a gentle slope, while the leeward has a steeper slope. From the slope of a sand dune, you can tell the wind direction.

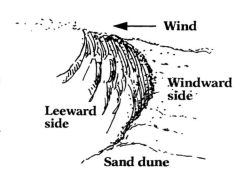

MATERIALS: sand, large piece of cardboard, water

- Make two small mountains of sand on the cardboard. Sprinkle water over one. Blow air over both. Have students notice how the dry mountain was moved away by the movement of air. This demonstrates wind erosion.

Wet sand   **Dry sand**

24. MAKING WAVES

Wind blowing over water surfaces causes waves. Their size depends on the wind speed. The top of the wave is a crest, while the bottom is a trough. The distance from either the crest or the trough to the water surface is wave height (amplitude). The greater the wave height, the greater the wave energy.

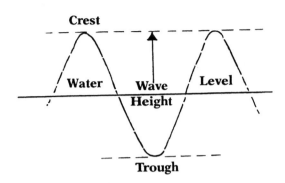

MATERIALS: shallow pan, water

- Blow air over a shallow pan of water to cause waves. Bottom-lit projection may show waves on the overhead, if you use a transparent pan.

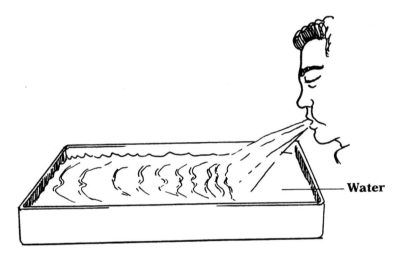

25. MINERALS IN OCEANS

Wind, water, glaciers, temperature, and chemical reactions cause erosion. The materials of erosion are carried by rivers into the oceans. The river water dissolves many minerals, then mixes with the salty ocean water, adding more minerals to the seawater.

MATERIALS: seawater, beaker, hot plate, salt, Bunsen burner, wire loop (platinum wire, if available), forceps

- Half-fill a beaker with seawater. If you do not have seawater, prepare a saturated solution of water with salt. Mix as much salt as the water will dissolve. Boil off the water and you will find a whitish crystalline residue in the beaker. These are the minerals dissolved in seawater. Test the residue for the presence of salt. (You will find another salt demonstration on page 9.)

- The flame test is used to identify salt. Sodium chloride (NaCl)—ordinary salt—is the most common mineral dissolved in the ocean. Sodium glows with a rich, bright yellow color. Make a wire loop, place on it some saltwater mineral residue, and place it over the flame. Use forceps to hold the wire. Platinum wire is preferred but not essential.

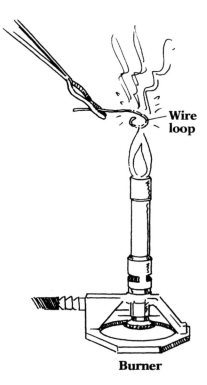

Wire loop

Burner

- Dip the wire loop in the seawater and repeat the flame test.

26. FOLDED ROCK LAYERS

Sedimentary rocks are usually formed in horizontal layers. Many times these rock layers show in cross section that they are bent upwards, as if folded at many different angles. Apparently the earth's crust pressures caused the layers to move upward. The movement of the earth is gradual and invisible, except during an earthquake. The earth's movement can be an uplift, drop, sideslip, or a combination of these. The earth's movements and earthquakes are caused by the motion of the earth's **tectonic plates**. Marine fossils that have been found on mountains thousands of feet high are evidence of this movement. The ancient city of Tehuanaca, in South America, has all the semblance of a seaport, yet it is over 10,000 feet above sea level.

MATERIALS: several sheets of colored paper

- Assemble a stack of many sheets of colored paper, each representing a layer. Take the entire stack and press together, causing center to bulge upward (**uplift**). This demonstrates the folding of rock layers.

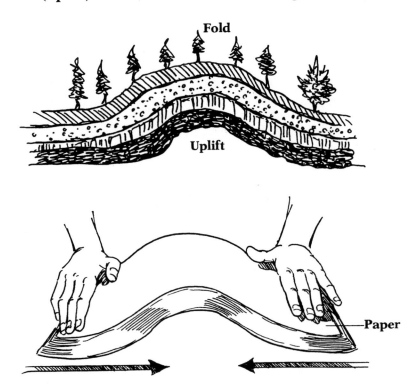

27. MAKING A FOSSIL

Animals that lived on earth before humans are called prehistoric. Mammoths (giant hairy elephants), dinosaurs, and saber-toothed cats are examples of prehistoric animals. Scientists find out about prehistoric animals from **fossils**: bones, footprints, shells, and actual animal or plant bodies. The majority of fossils are found in sedimentary rocks, which at some time were under the ocean. Water entering the rock may have dissolved the bones, but their impression remained in the rock. If this impression was filled with minerals and other debris, the filler formed the exact copy of the original bone, animal, or shell. This is called the cast.

MATERIALS: seashell or small bone, clay, small containers, mixing beaker, plaster of Paris, water, teaspoon

- Make your own fossil overnight.

1. Place the clay on the bottom of one small container.

2. Press into it the shell or bone, making a mold.

3. Remove the shell or bone.

4. In the other container, prepare some plaster of Paris by adding water and mixing until it is creamy and barely flowing.

5. Pour the plaster of Paris into the mold, the impression of the shell or bone.

6. Let the plaster of Paris harden overnight.

7. Gently tap and remove the fossil cast the next day.

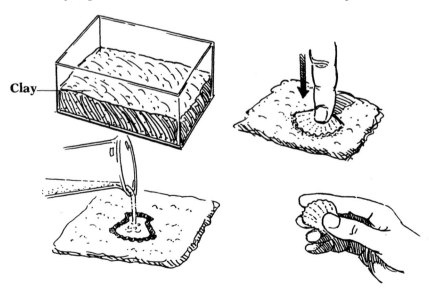

Clay

28. MAKING CHARCOAL—A FOSSIL FUEL

Fossil fuels were formed in prehistoric times from the remains of living things. Common fossil fuels are coal, natural gas, and liquid petroleum. Charcoal, a form of the element carbon, is formed when materials burn and lack sufficient oxygen to totally oxidize (burn).

MATERIALS: test tube, test tube holder, stand, Bunsen burner, wood splints, matches

- Place several wood splints in a test tube and hold the test tube up with a stand. Tip the test tube up slightly. Heat the test tube until the splints inside turn black. While this process is ongoing, take a lit splint and place it at the mouth of the test tube. It will burn because the by-product of changing the wood into charcoal is a gas similar to natural gas.

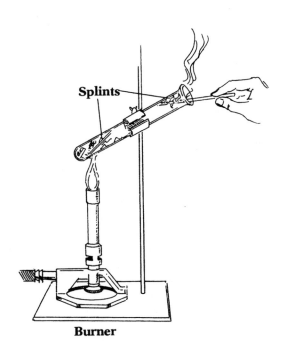

Splints

Burner

29. AIR OCCUPIES SPACE

The **atmosphere** is the 500-mile-high ocean of air surrounding the earth. Most of its air molecules are concentrated in the lower 75 miles. As one goes higher, air pressure drops and there is less oxygen. Air takes up space. Air is a mixture composed of several gases:

1. Nitrogen 78%

2. Oxygen 21%

3. Argon 0.94%

4. Carbon dioxide 0.04%

5. Helium, krypton, neon, xenon 0.02%

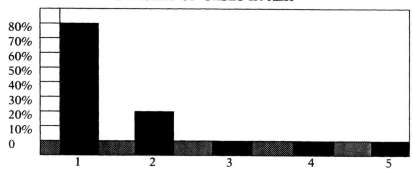

PERCENT OF GASES IN AIR

MATERIALS: large plastic bag

• Fill the plastic bag with air, close it, and feel how air fills the bag. Air does occupy space.

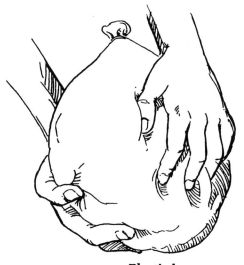

Plastic bag

30. AIR HAS MASS

MATERIALS: balloon, balance

- Inflate the balloon with air and place it on the balance. Balance it. Release the air and place the balloon back on the balance. It became lighter. This proves that air has mass.

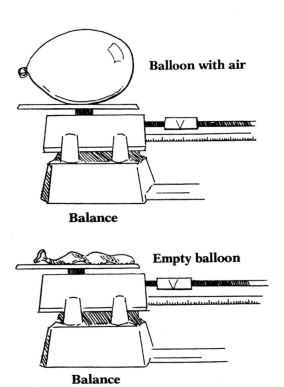

Balloon with air

Balance

Empty balloon

Balance

31. FIRE NEEDS OXYGEN

To have a fire, one needs fuel, oxygen, and kindling temperature.

MATERIALS: small aluminum dish or pie tin, birthday candle, water, empty jar, matches

- Light the candle and drip some wax into the dish. Then place the candle in the wax so that it stays upright. Fill the dish with water. Cover the candle with the jar. Notice that the candle goes out after a short while. It has used up all the oxygen in the jar. Fire needs oxygen.

- Remove the jar and relight the candle. Wet your fingers. Squeeze the flame of the candle. It goes out. You have deprived the flame of essential oxygen.

32. AIR IS 20% OXYGEN

MATERIALS: pie tin or aluminum plate, water, graduated cylinder, candle, matches

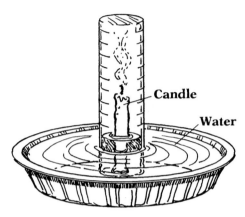

Candle

Water

- Light the candle and drip several drops of candle wax into the plate. Then place the candle in the wax so that it stays upright. Fill the dish nearly full of water. Place the inverted graduated cylinder over the candle. Notice the level of water inside the cylinder. After a short time, the candle goes out. Notice how the water has risen inside the graduated cylinder. The rise is about one-fifth or 20% of the inside volume of gas. This confirms that oxygen makes up 21% of air.

33. FIRE MAKES CARBON DIOXIDE

MATERIALS: test tube, limewater, small piece of paper, matches

- Place a small piece of lit paper in the mouth of a test tube containing limewater. Shake the test tube and observe how the limewater turns milky. This indicates the presence of carbon dioxide, a by-product of fire.

Burning paper

Limewater

34. CONDUCTION OF HEAT

When heat is added to objects, molecules begin to vibrate faster and further apart. The heat energy is transferred from molecule to molecule. This is **conduction** of heat. Earth, after being warmed by the sun, passes its heat by conduction to the air.

MATERIALS: Bunsen burner, piece of metal or old silverware

- Heat a strip of metal or an old piece of silverware on one end and have students notice how the other end becomes gradually warmer

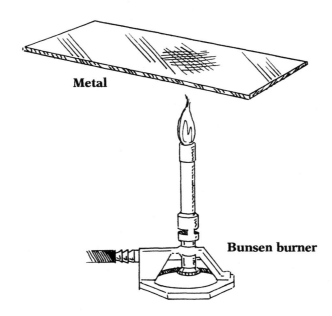

Metal

Bunsen burner

35. RADIATION OF HEAT #1

The sun emits many forms of energy that travel out to the universe in waves. Among the many energy forms are invisible **infrared rays**, which have longer wavelengths than visible light. These are rays of heat energy. This method of heat energy transfer is radiation.

CAUTION! Advise students not to place their hands too close to the bulb.

MATERIALS: light with bulb

• Turn on the lightbulb and let it glow for a few minutes. Have your students feel the heat radiated by the bulb.

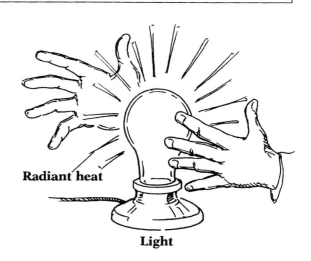

36. RADIATION OF HEAT #2

MATERIALS: lamp with heat bulb, glass of water, thermometer

• Place the lamp with heat bulb above the glass of water. Place the thermometer in the glass. Notice the water temperature. Let the heat from the bulb heat the water. Take the temperature every few minutes to show a change.

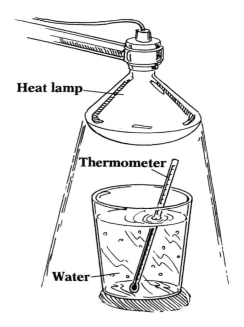

37. DETECTING HEAT WITH A RADIOMETER

MATERIALS: radiometer, light with bulb, infrared passing filter

- Place the radiometer a few inches from the lightbulb. Show students how the radiometer spins around when exposed to the light and heat of the lightbulb. Next, show students how the infrared passing filter blocks all visible light and prevents them from seeing the bulb at all. Now, place the infrared passing filter between the light and the radiometer. The radiometer will continue to turn, even though no light reaches it. This demonstrates that there must be some other form of energy, invisible to the eye, that reaches the radiometer and makes it move. This energy is infrared rays—heat.

Light   **Infrared passing filter**

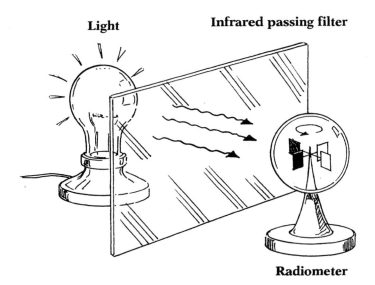

Radiometer

38. WARM AIR RISES: CONVECTION

Warm air rises causing air currents, or winds. Warm-water streams move through the oceans and make ocean currents. Movement of warmer substances up and colder ones down is **convection**. Warmer substances are lighter because their molecules are further apart and fewer molecules occupy the space they took up when the substances were colder. This lessening of mass makes the substances more buoyant (floating) in the ocean of air or water.

MATERIALS: two large paper shopping bags, string, adhesive tape, two metersticks, lamp

- Hang the two inverted (upside-down) shopping bags on one meterstick with string. Balance the bags so that they are as far apart as possible. Hang this meterstick, at its center of balance from another meterstick that rests between two student desks. Place the lamp below one bag and turn on the lamp. As the heat from the bulb heats up the air in the bag, the bag will appear to be lighter and will rise.

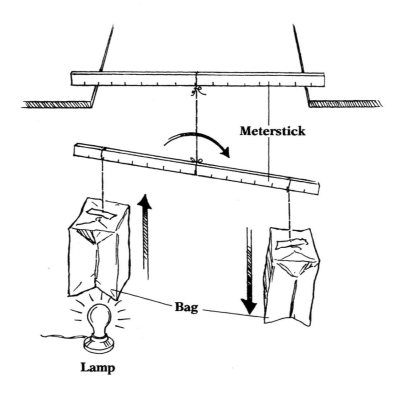

39. Warm Water Rises: Convection

Ocean water is warmest near the surface and gets colder with depth, forming a thermal gradient. Different temperature zones have unique animal and plant life because oceanic inhabitants are temperature sensitive. On maps, contours with the same temperatures are **thermoclines**. One of the best-known oceanic currents is the Gulf Stream. It begins in the Gulf of Mexico, flows northeastward across the Atlantic, and passes by and warms up the west coast of Africa and western Europe.

MATERIALS: fish tank nearly full of water, food coloring, convection jar, hot water

(A convection jar can be built from a baby food jar. Punch two holes in its lid and insert the cylindrical portions of two plastic eye droppers. Insert one to be as deep as the jar and place the other above the lid. Seal them with florist clay or a heat-melt glue gun. Prepare several jars for later use.)

- Fill the convection jar with warm water and add several drops of food coloring. Cover the jar and place it gently on the bottom of the fish tank. (A large transparent jar can be used as a substitute for the fish tank.) You will observe immediate convection currents as the colored water moves upwards. This activity is visible both in the tank and inside the convection bottle. Later, you may wish to repeat the demonstration, using a different color. Soon you will have a water tank with colored layers to represent thermoclines.

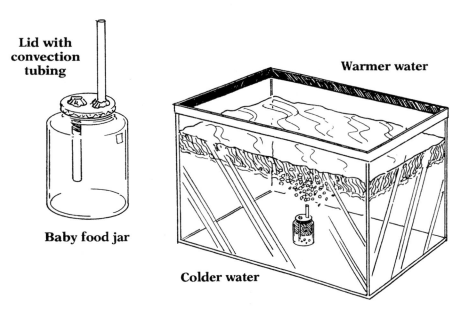

Lid with convection tubing

Baby food jar

Warmer water

Colder water

40. INVERSION LAYER AND SMOG

Thermal inversion develops when warm air masses form a blanketlike cover over colder air masses. The trapped underlying air masses become polluted and, through photochemical reaction (the chemicals in the air react with sunshine), smog develops. Smog is a major ecological and health problem of most large cities.

- Use Demonstration 39, Warm Water Rises: Convection, to illustrate this concept.

41. LAND HEATS AND COOLS MORE QUICKLY THAN WATER

The sun heats up both the continental land masses and the oceans. The weather and climate on earth are directly dependent on this heat energy transfer and so are all the secondary phenomena that accompany it, such as winds, tornadoes, hurricanes, rain, snow, and oceanic waves. Continental masses heat up and cool more quickly than water masses. During the day, flat lands are colder than the adjacent hills. Air flows from the valleys to the hills, from a region of higher pressure to one of lower pressure, causing a valley breeze. At night, the hills are colder than the valley and the reverse is true. The heavier (denser) mountain air flows down to the valleys, causing a mountain breeze.

MATERIALS: two containers, soil, water, two thermometers, lamp (optional)

- Fill both containers about three-quarters full—one with soil and the other with water. Place a thermometer in both. Place both containers in sunshine or under a lamp. Measure the temperatures of both at the start and after about 25 minutes. The soil will be warmer than the water.

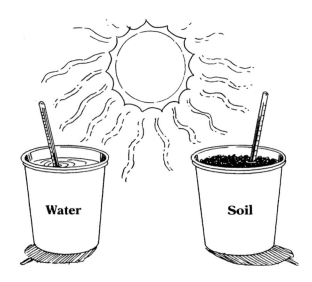

42. SUBSTANCES AND SPECIFIC HEAT CAPACITY

Different materials need different amounts of heat energy to rise to the same temperature. Temperature is a measure of heat in a material, and indirectly is a measure of molecular speed.

MATERIALS: three identical pint jars, powdered iron, sand, water (or your choice of materials), three thermometers

- Half-fill all three containers with powdered iron, sand, and water. Place a thermometer in each container and expose them to the sun. Measure the temperatures after 25 minutes. The iron will have the highest temperature, next the sand, and next the water. In more advanced science, the amount of heat absorption is **specific heat capacity**. Every material has its own specific heat capacity.

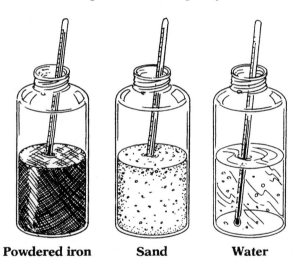

Powdered iron   **Sand**   **Water**

43. AIR PRESSURE IS EXERTED ON ALL SIDES

The pressure of air is exerted in all directions. In the following activities, some students may erroneously assume that surface tension holds the board in place.

MATERIALS: glass, water, piece of cardboard, sink or basin

- Fill a glass with water to the brim. Then place a piece of cardboard on it. Invert and notice how the water does not fall out. The pressure of air keeps the cardboard in place. Do this demonstration over a sink or basin, just in case of problems.

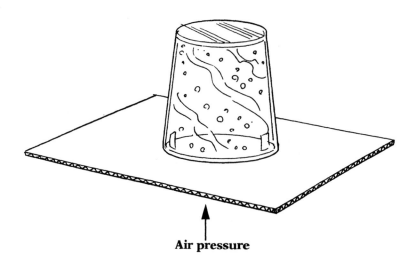

Air pressure

44. AIR PRESSURE AND EGG IN AND OUT OF BOTTLE

When energy is unbalanced (i.e., higher versus lower pressure), be it osmotic, electrical (voltage), or physical (air pressure), energy flows from the region of higher pressure to the lower one until a balance (equilibrium) is attained. If a space capsule loses its pressure integrity, life-supporting air escapes out to the vacuum of space with fatal consequences for the spacefarers. On planet earth, the pressure of the ocean of air above it (atmosphere) is 14.7 pounds per square inch. This pressure is sufficient to crush any container with vacuum inside it, unless it is specifically designed to withstand these forces, like Magdeburg hemispheres.

MATERIALS: shelled hard-boiled egg, birthday candle, large bottle or jar (with mouth barely smaller than the egg), matches

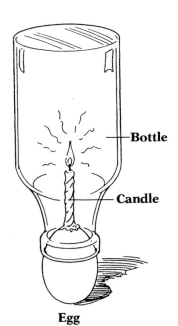

Bottle

Candle

Egg

- Insert the candle into either end of the egg and light it. Place the candle inside the bottle and seal the opening with the egg. As the candle burns the oxygen, 20% of the inside gas, the bottle will have a region of lower pressure. Eventually the egg will squeeze into the bottle. Be careful to use one hand only, as soon as you have positioned the egg, so that students can see how things happen.

- To remove the egg, hold the bottle with its opening down and blow air into it. As you blow, gravity will hold the egg at the opening, maintaining a seal. The air above the egg will gain more pressure and the egg will squeeze out.

45. AIR PRESSURE AND SODA CAN

MATERIALS: empty soda can, tablespoon, small pan, water, forceps, Bunsen burner

- Place a tablespoon of water into an empty soda can. Fill the pan nearly full. Heat the soda can on a Bunsen burner until steam begins to escape from the pop top. Rapidly invert the can and place its top in the pan of water. The cooling of the air inside the can will create enough air pressure difference for the air pressure to crush the can. The water inside the can creates steam. Steam contains fewer molecules than the equivalent volume of hot air, thus creating a greater vacuum.

46. AIR PRESSURE CRUSHES A CAN

The pressure of air will crush any container that has vacuum inside it unless it is built to withstand air pressure of 14.7 pounds per square inch.

MATERIALS: Bunsen burner, tablespoon, small amount of water, string, stand with ring, empty gallon can. The can needs to be clean on the inside, preferably new.

CAUTION! Do not use a can that has held flammable liquids.

- Follow these steps:

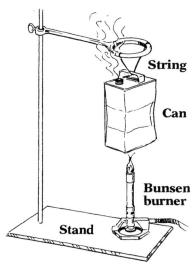

1. Tie a piece of string to the can. Then hang the can from the ring.

2. Place the ring high enough to allow for the Bunsen burner.

3. Place a tablespoon of water inside the can.

4. Heat the can until white vapor starts coming out from the can. While heating, move the burner around, so no part of the can burns through.

5. Stop heating. Quickly close the can with its lid.

6. Let it stand. Spin it lightly. The can will implode gradually.

7. To speed up the process, cool the can by spraying it with water.

47. AIR PRESSURE HOLDS UP A COLUMN OF WATER

The pressure of air can hold up a column of water almost 34 feet high (almost 10 meters). This is true at sea level at standard temperature and pressure (STP.) At higher altitudes, the pressure drops, since there is less air above. The lowering of air pressure lowers the boiling point of liquids. Certain foods that will cook at 100°C at sea level will remain raw despite long cooking in the mountains. Pressure cookers help in these situations. By increasing the internal pot pressure, pressure cookers increase the boiling point and allow foods to be cooked sooner. Pressure caps on car radiators increase the boiling point of the coolant. This allows car cooling systems to boil at higher temperatures and absorb more heat energy from the engine before boiling over.

MATERIALS: glass, container, water

- Fill the container nearly full of water. Place the glass in the pan, submerge it, and make sure that the glass is full of water. Invert the glass and pull it gently up from the water, but stop before you reach the top edges of the glass. The water will stay on the inside of the glass due to the pressure of air.

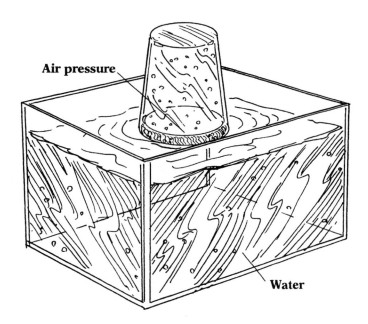

48. MAKING AN ANEROID BAROMETER

An **aneroid barometer** does not contain any liquid. It is usually made from a small can with one very thin side that moves in or out with the slightest changes in air pressure. A pointer is connected to this thin part of the can and it points along a scale. The aneroid barometer in this demonstration is easy to assemble. It consists of a vacuum-packed coffee can and a pointer that magnifies the subtle caving in or expansion of the can. It is a mechanical amplifier. The rising air pressure is a predictor of fair weather, while the dropping pressure indicates bad weather. You may either calibrate your barometer against another one or listen to weather forecasts for your reference points. In making your own weather forecasts include other data such as temperature, moisture, and clouds.

MATERIALS: one piece of 1- × 6- × 36-inch board (the base), 1- × 2- × 12-inch stick (scale support), ¼-inch dowel 33 inches in length (pivoting pointer), pin (pointer tip), 1- × 1- × 12-inch stick (pivot upright), unopened can of coffee or any other vacuum-packed product (of similar size), wood glue, screws, 6-inch long stiff wire, soldering iron, solder, drill, measuring tape, pencil

- Follow these steps:

1. Mark the centerline on the base board (Carefully examine the illustration.)

2. Fasten the coffee can securely on the centerline by gluing its bottom or securing it with screws overlapping the bottom rim (without breaking the vacuum of the can).

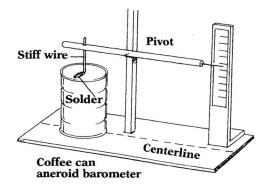

Coffee can
aneroid barometer

3. Take the piece of stiff wire and bend it into the shape of an L. Solder the short end to the center of the coffee can so that the longer end is perpendicular to the top of the can.

4. Fasten the pivot upright stick one-eighth of an inch off center to act as a pivot arm support.

5. Drill a hole about three inches from one end of the dowel. Secure the dowel into the pivot arm support with a screw. Make certain that the pivot arm is free to move and installed on the center line.

6. Install the scale support on the opposite end of the board. Offset it from the centerline to allow for the pivot arm. Secure it with wood glue and a screw from below.

7. Place the pin on the end of the pivot arm to act as a pointer.

8. Connect the stiff wire to the pivot arm in the horizontal position.

9. Make a scale and fasten it on the support.

49. THE WEIGHT OF AIR PRESSURE

If you take a square inch and go upwards for 500 miles, you will have a volume of air 500 miles high and one square inch on the bottom. The total mass of this air is 14.7 pounds. Air exerts a pressure of 14.7 pounds per square inch on the bottom of this ocean of air, the atmosphere. If you go to the mountains, the air column becomes shorter and therefore there is less mass and less air pressure.

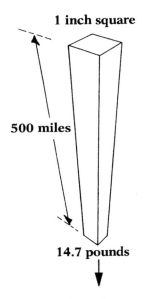

1 inch square

500 miles

14.7 pounds

MATERIALS: three or four bricks, marker, ruler

- Ask one student who is wearing white, smooth-soled shoes to volunteer for this demonstration. Ask the student to sit in front of the class and place his or her foot on a desk, so that everyone can see the sole of the shoe. Draw a one-inch square on the sole.
Now that everyone has seen one square inch, have the students line up and pass each other the stack of bricks. Comment that this is like the pressure of air on our bodies, on each square inch. Without atmospheric pressure, our bodies would behave as many science fiction movies have depicted most vividly.

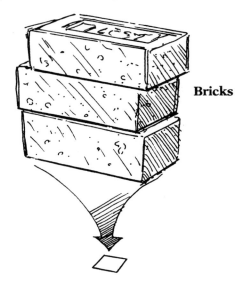

Bricks

50. WIND DIRECTION: MAKING A WIND VANE

The direction of the wind is an important component of weather. Airports have air socks and wind vanes. Weather forecasters launch helium balloons to find the direction of wind. By combining the wind vane with a compass, one can establish wind direction. You may wish to mount the assembled vane on the roof or other elevated place at your school.

MATERIALS: roller skate or skateboard wheel, dowel, 3-inch bolt (fits inside wheel axle), three nuts, aluminum sheet metal (or pie tin), small wood base (6 × 6 inches)

- Follow these steps:

1. See illustration for help.

2. In the center of the wood base, drill a hole wider and deeper than the bolt with a nut on it. The bolt must be able to turn freely in this hole after all the nuts have been installed.

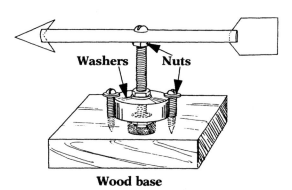

3. Prepare an arrow and a tail from the aluminum sheeting or pie plate. Assemble the weather vane by attaching the arrow and the tail to the dowel. For best results, make the tail at least twice the size of the pointer. Drill a hole in the dowel and place it on the bolt. Install a nut to fasten this assembly to the bolt head. Mount the support bolt in the center of the wheel, with nuts on both sides.

4. Mount the skate wheel centered over the hole in the base, so that the assembly can turn freely. The wheel will have a real ball bearing for ease of turning.

5. Mount the wheel with screws and large washers.

6. Occasionally oil the wheel.

7. A less sensitive wind vane can be built using a small block, a stick, some cardboard for the arrow and tail, a center pivot made with a nail and washers above and below the stick. This primitive model will work only in more substantial winds.

51. WATER VAPOR

Water exists in the atmosphere in the form of gas, or water vapor. Most of it comes from the **evaporation** of the oceans. Plants and animals add water to the air. Plants add water to the air through the process of **transpiration**.

MATERIALS: plant, plastic bag, sponge, water, mirror, coffeepot

- Breathe on a mirror. Show the **condensation** of water vapor.

- Demonstrate evaporation: Moisten a sponge and wet your chalkboard. Let students observe how it dries up.

- Demonstrate transpiration: Cover a plant with a plastic bag, place it in the sun for about 15 minutes, and observe the moisture condensing on the inside.

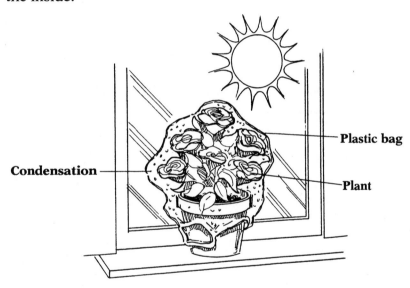

- Lift the lid of a heated coffeepot and show the water vapor going up.

52. ABSOLUTE AND RELATIVE HUMIDITY

The amount of water vapor in the air around us is humidity. Since air can hold varying amounts of water, the true amount of water in the air is **absolute humidity.** The amount of water present in the air compared to the maximum amount possible is **relative humidity.** High relative humidity can make people uncomfortable because their perspiration will not evaporate; they feel warmer than they would at the same temperature in less-humid conditions. When the temperature is adjusted for the relative humidity, it is **apparent temperature.**

- Using the temperature and humidity from your local weather station, convert your temperature to apparent temperature, using the table below. If the air temperature is 85°F and the relative humidity is 60%, the apparent temperature is 90°F. Some weather forecasts also refer to the apparent temperature as the comfort index.

APPARENT TEMPERATURE F° CHART

AIR TEMPERATURE degrees Fahrenheit

RELATIVE HUMIDITY	70	75	80	85	90	95	100	105	110	115	120
0%	64	69	73	78	83	87	91	95	99	103	107
10%	65	70	75	80	85	90	95	100	105	111	116
20%	66	72	77	82	87	93	99	105	112	120	130
30%	67	73	78	84	90	96	104	113	123	135	148
40%	68	74	79	86	93	101	110	123	137	151	
50%	69	75	81	88	96	107	120	135	150		
60%	70	76	82	90	100	114	132	149			
70%	70	77	85	93	106	124	144				
80%	71	78	86	97	113	136					
90%	71	79	88	102	122						
100%	72	80	91	108							

53. RELATIVE HUMIDITY MEASUREMENT: MAKING A PSYCHROMETER

The relative humidity measurement is made with a psychrometer. The instrument consists of two thermometers on a board that can be spun around (assembly described below). The bulb of one of the thermometers is covered by wet cotton. When the instrument is spinned, the water of the wet bulb will evaporate. The rate of its evaporation will be a function of the humidity of air. As water evaporates, it will cool the thermometer. By knowing the temperature of the dry thermometer and the difference between the dry and wet thermometer temperatures, one can find out the relative humidity by using the chart that follows. For a complete metric relative-humidity chart, obtain U.S. Weather Bureau Bulletin #1071.

MATERIALS: small board, two thermometers, glue, small amount of cotton cloth, rubber band, small handle (dowel), screw, screwdriver

- Follow these steps:

1. Glue the thermometers on the board (see illustration).

2. Place the cloth around one thermometer bulb and secure it with a tiny rubber band.

3. Attach the dowel with the screw.

- Measure the relative humidity by using the psychrometer and the chart provided on the following page. The chart is accurate for a barometric pressure of 74.27 centimeters Hg and temperatures above -10°C. Between 77.5 and 71 centimeters Hg, the values will be less than the error of observation.

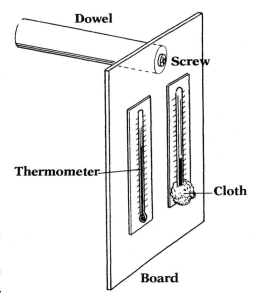

RELATIVE HUMIDITY % CHART

Difference between wet and dry temperatures °C

AIR TEMPERATURE DRY °C	1	2	3	4	5	6	7	8	9	10	11	12
0	81	64	46	29	13							
5	86	72	58	45	33	20	7					
10	88	77	66	55	44	34	24	15	6			
15	90	80	71	61	53	44	36	27	20	13	6	
20	91	83	74	66	59	51	44	37	31	24	18	12
25	92	84	77	70	63	57	50	44	39	33	28	22
30	93	86	79	73	67	61	55	50	44	39	35	28
35	94	87	81	75	69	64	59	54	49	44	40	36
40	94	88	82	77	72	67	62	57	53	48	44	40

Relative Humidity %

54. THE DEW POINT

Water vapor condenses back into a liquid when the temperature drops. The point of transition from a gas to a liquid is the **dew point**. As the temperature drops, air becomes saturated with water vapor, because cold air can hold less vapor than warm air. The fine water condensation that first appears is dew. Water freezes at 0°C or +32°F. When the humidity in the air is low, the dew point drops below the freezing temperature of water. If the air temperature drops to the dew point, the water vapor in the air will change into frost (ice), not water.

MATERIALS: thermometer, metal can, water, ice

Thermometer

Ice cubes

Can

- Half-fill the can with water. Place the thermometer in the can. Add ice cubes and stir gently. When condensation appears on the outside of the can, read the thermometer. This is the dew point for your room air at this time.

55. HUMIDITY MEASUREMENT: MAKING A HYGROMETER

A **hygrometer** measures humidity in the air.

MATERIALS: stand with clamp, glass rod or tubing, human hair, small washer or button, toothpick (pointed), glue, index card, cardboard, masking tape

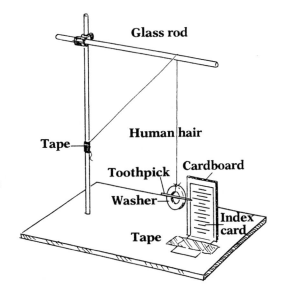

- Attach a small washer or button to the end of a washed human hair. Hang the hair from the glass rod and fasten it to the stand with some adhesive tape. The length of the hair will vary with humidity and the little weight will move up and down. Glue a toothpick to the flat side of the washer. Place an index card on a support made from cardboard, behind the toothpick, and slowly calibrate the hygrometer according to daily weather forecasts—or use a psychrometer.

56. CLOUD IN A BOTTLE

Clouds form when air pressures drop, causing the temperature to drop. Water vapor begins to condense. For water vapor to condense, tiny particles, called **condensation nuclei**, must be present. These particles—dust, smoke, or salt—become the center of droplets that form a cloud.

MATERIALS: pressure flask, stopper with two holes, small glass tube, rubber hose, hose clamp, steel valve stem from car or bicycle tire, tire pump, water, matches, sheet of black paper, flashlight, graduated cylinder, water

- Prepare the stopper by inserting the tire valve stem through one hole and a small piece of glass tubing through the other one. On the outside end of the glass tubing, place a small piece of rubber hose and clamp it. Pour 25 milliliters of water in the flask. Light a match and place it inside the bottle for a few seconds so that some smoke remains inside. Cover the bottle and pump air into it to increase its internal pressure. Behind the bottle, place a large sheet of black paper and shine a light through the bottle. Open the clamp and let the air pressure inside the bottle drop. With the drop of pressure, the temperature inside the bottle drops. You will observe a cloud in the bottle. The smoke particles acted as condensation nuclei. (Optional: If you pack dry ice around the flask, some of the cloud will precipitate as snow.)

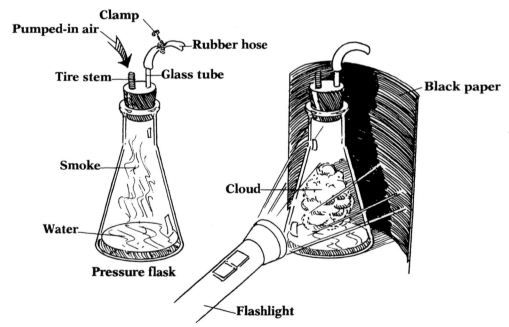

57. TORNADO SIMULATOR #1

Tornadoes form when warm, moist air masses meet with cold air. Light and moist air rises up while the cold air moves down. The path of the warm air is like a funnel, spiraling upwards and spinning around. As tornadoes move along the land, their spinning centers, being regions of very low pressure, suck up anything on the ground, with devastating effects.

MATERIALS: two plastic 1-liter soda bottles, two hose washers, tornado device, water

You can buy a tornado demonstrator for a few dollars from most scientific supply houses. Edmunds Scientific (101 E. Gloucester Pike, Barrington, NJ 08007) is a resource.

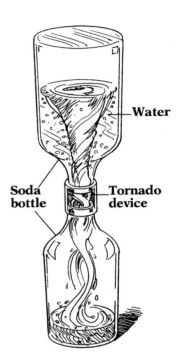

- Insert the tornado device between two empty plastic 1-liter soda bottles. Place a hose washer on both ends of this plastic connector before screwing on the bottles. One bottle will be filled with water. Invert the assembly so that the water is in the upper bottle. Spin the assembly clockwise several times. The liquid will assume the shape of a tornado.

58. TORNADO SIMULATOR #2

If you wish a larger demonstration machine for a tornado than the one in Demonstration 57, build the following assembly. Exact measurements are not given in the materials list so that you can make the demonstrator box any size.

MATERIALS: three glass panes (sides), board (side), black matte paint, two square boards (base and cover), drill, high-intensity light, hot plate, flat pan, water

- Refer to the illustrations and follow these steps:

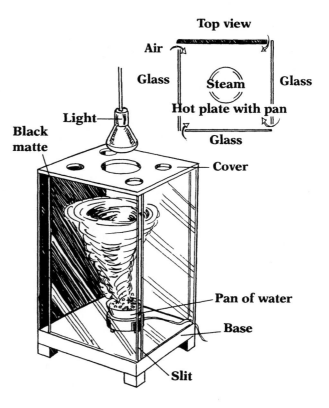

1. Paint the nonglass box side a flat black. Secure the four sides to the wooden base, allowing half-inch slits as shown in the illustration. The painted surface should face inwards.

2. Drill a large hole in the center of the cover for a high-intensity light to shine in. Drill at least four smaller holes to allow water vapor to escape.

3. Place a hot plate on the base with a pan of water.

4. To simulate a tornado, boil the water. Ambient air will enter through the side slits and create a whirlpool effect. Shine a high-intensity light through the cover hole to illuminate the demonstration.

59. MAKING A SIMPLE REFRACTING TELESCOPE

The telescope was invented by a Dutch optician in 1608. Galileo Galilei was the first person to make a large model. With this telescope, he observed the moon and the planets in the solar system. Galileo built a **refracting telescope**, one that uses two **convex** lenses. The convex lens is thicker in the middle than the edge, like a drop of water.

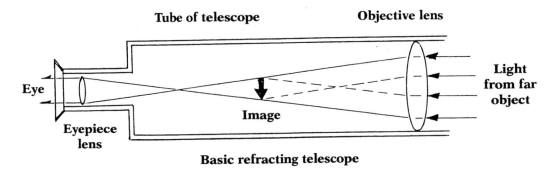

Basic refracting telescope

MATERIALS: two magnifying glasses

- Take one magnifying lens and observe an object in the distance. Move the lens closer or further away until you have a sharp image. The image will be inverted and smaller. Take the second magnifying glass and place it in front of your eye. Move this lens back and forth slowly until you see the object clearly. The object will appear larger.

60. MAKING A SIMPLE MIRROR TELESCOPE

Mirror telescopes (reflecting telescopes) offer several advantages over refracting telescopes: They are smaller and gather more light. Isaac Newton built the first reflecting telescope in 1671. Each type of telescope has its own advantages.

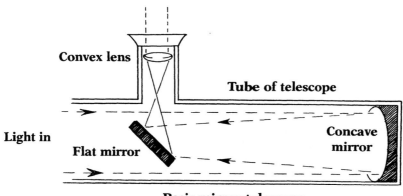

Basic mirror telescope

MATERIALS: lightbulb in lamp base, magnifying lens, mirror with concave surface (magnifying mirror with two sides, used for makeup and shaving)

• Place the light on a table in a darkened room. Use the concave surface of the mirror to reflect the lightbulb on the wall. By moving the mirror slightly, try to get a sharp image on the wall. Observe the image of the bulb on the wall through the magnifying glass. By moving the magnifying glass around you can make the bulb appear bigger.

61. MAKING A SIMPLE SPECTROMETER

Light is the sum of all the colors of light (the rainbow). A rainbow breaks the light of the sun into its basic colors. A **prism** or a **diffraction grating** does the same thing. A diffraction grating is a thin plastic sheet that has thousands of fine lines ruled into it. These lines break up light like a prism. When an element's flame is viewed through a **spectroscope**, a type of spectrometer, it shows a **spectrum** or band that is unique to it. In this manner substances can be identified accurately. By combining a spectroscope with a telescope, a scientist can find out the composition, size, direction of travel, and age of a star.

MATERIALS: cardboard tube, diffraction grating, piece of black paper, tape, rubber band, razor blade, bright light

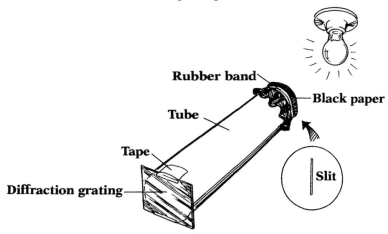

- Tape the diffraction grating on one end of the tube. Using a rubber band, cover the other end with the black paper. Cut a very fine slit through the center two-thirds of the paper. Point the slit toward a bright light and slowly rotate the tube until you see the spectrum.

CAUTION! Do not allow anyone to look at the sun.

---

62. BRIGHTNESS OF STARS: MAGNITUDE

The brightness of a star is the light given off by its hot gases. **Magnitude** is a measure of a star's apparent brightness. If two stars of the same size and brightness are located so that one is near and the other far away, the closer one will appear brighter and have a greater magnitude. Less bright does not mean necessarily smaller. Imagine a car moving toward you at night. Its headlights are dim at a great distance but are very bright as the car passes you. Star life cycles go from blue to yellow to red color. Blue is the hottest and youngest, yellow is middle age, and red is a nearly dying star. Color is judged by the temperature of a hot metal that emits the same spectrum, in Kelvin degrees, as the color spectrum in question. Note that electronic flash units have color temperatures in their specifications. Photographic films are also rated for their response to specific color temperatures. The combination of spectroscopy and radioastronomy (wave analysis) are the principal tools used by modern astronomers. These are used also through observations made in deep space by a host of robotics devices including earth-orbiting telescopes. Data is gathered for visible light, X rays, infrared rays, ultraviolet rays, and other energy forms.

MATERIALS: variac or light dimmer, lightbulb, lightbulb base, Bunsen burner, forceps, sewing needle, two light bases with two bulbs of different wattage

- Set up the variac to provide power for the bulb base. By turning the variac control, you can make the bulb glow brighter and dimmer. A dim bulb is not nearly as hot as a bright one.

- *Alternate:* Heat the sewing needle and have students observe how it gets brighter as it gets hotter.

- Show students two lightbulbs of different wattage. The bulb with more watts is larger. The same is true for stars; at the same distance, the star with greater brightness is larger than a star with less brightness.

100 watts

25 watts

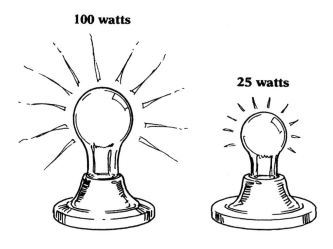

63. PARALLAX

Parallax is the relative motion of an object seen against a fixed background, when it is viewed from two different points. Astronomers use parallax to find distances to the nearer stars. Parallax explains why sometimes people take photographs with heads partially cut off. The camera sees the person through the lens, while the photographer sees the person through a separate viewfinder. This is one of the reasons why single lens reflex cameras are so popular. These cameras view through the photographic lens and introduce no parallax error.

- Ask your students to look at an object (picture, clock, etc.) across the room with both eyes open. Have them hold a finger away from their bodies in front of a specific point on this object. Have them close the left eye first, then open it and close the right eye. As they do so, the finger will appear to move for one eye but not for the other one. This apparent motion is parallax. The eye for which the finger did not move is the dominant eye.

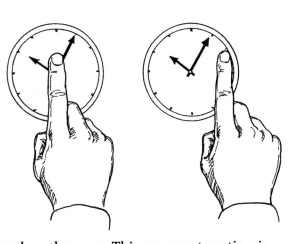

64. ASTRONOMICAL UNIT

The measurement of distance in space involves enormous numbers. To better describe great distances within our own solar system, astronomers use the distance from the earth to the sun, about 93 million miles (150 million kilometers), as 1 AU (**astronomical unit**.)

MATERIALS: several rolls of adding machine tape, metersticks, adhesive tape

- Ask student teams to show the distances of the planets from the sun by marking off the astronomical units for each planet on adding machine tape. Use one meter to represent each AU. Have students step outside the classroom and stretch out the tapes.

PLANET	DISTANCE AU
Mercury	0.39
Venus	0.72
Earth	1.00
Mars	1.52
Jupiter	5.2
Saturn	9.5
Uranus	19.2
Neptune	30.1
Pluto	39.5

- An alternate activity is to measure the distances in astronomical units out on the playground. Have individual students act as markers by standing at each planetary position. Select an object to represent the position of the sun.

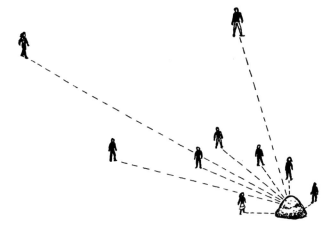

65. Calculating a Light-Year

The **light-year** is an astronomical unit of measurement used to measure distances to the stars. The light of the sun takes $8\frac{1}{3}$ minutes to reach us. A light-year is the distance that light travels in one year: 9.46 trillion kilometers (5.88 trillion miles). Light travels at 299,792.4562 kilometers (186,282 miles) per second ± 1.1 meter per second. For ordinary calculations, this is rounded off to 300,000 kilometers per second.

MATERIALS: calculator

- Have your students calculate the distance that light travels in one year. The chart is for your reference.

Time	Seconds	Travel Distance of Light (in kilometers)
1 second	1	300,000
1 minute	60	18,000,000
1 hour	3,600	1,080,000,000
1 day	86,400	25,920,000,000
1 week	604,800	181,440,000,000
1 year	220,900,000	9,460,800,000,000

66. BLOCKING THE SUN'S ULTRAVIOLET RAYS

The sun sends out enormous amounts of energy. Earth receives about $\frac{1}{2000000000}$ (one two-billionth) of the sun's energy, despite the filtering out by our atmosphere. Sunshine contains invisible **ultraviolet** (UV) rays that can burn the skin and cause cancer. To prevent this, one needs to use sunscreen. Ultraviolet rays are radiation with a wavelength slightly longer than X rays.

MATERIALS: salad oil, sunscreen, two pieces of colored paper of different colors

- Cover one half of a piece of colored paper with salad oil, the other half with sunscreen. Expose the paper to the sun for one morning. Repeat with another color. The sunscreen will prevent the fading of the color. Keep a piece of reference paper away from light for later comparison.

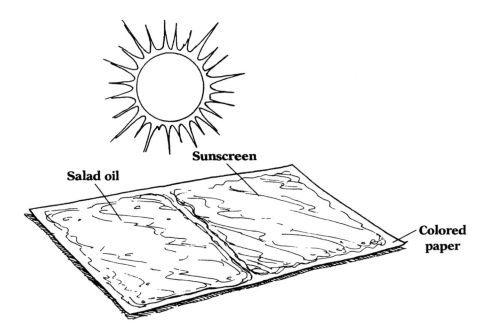

67. VIEWING THE SUN AND SOLAR ECLIPSES

Viewing the sun is desirable at times, especially during solar eclipses. Quality telescopes are equipped with solar viewing plates and solar filters. You need to check, if you buy a filter, that it has the UL (United Laboratories) seal of approval. Many inexpensive filters heat up and break during observations, with subsequent damage to the viewer's eyes. Looking directly at the sun will damage the eyes. Looking at the sun through several layers of exposed photographic film is also harmful, because infrared rays (heat) will go through to cause severe and permanent eye damage. The following pinhole projector provides a safe way to observe the sun and solar eclipses.

MATERIALS: shoe box, index card, needle, adhesive tape

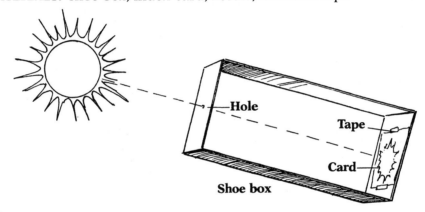

- Remove the cover of the shoe box . With the needle punch a small hole near the middle of one end of the box. Tape an index card inside the box at the opposite end of the hole. Point the hole toward the sun and move the box until an image of the sun appears on the index card.

CAUTION! Warn your students never to look directly at the sun.

68. ECLIPSE OF THE SUN

A solar eclipse occurs when the moon, in its rotation around the earth, is in a position between the sun and the earth, thus blocking some of the sun's rays. If only part of the sun's face is blocked, it is a partial eclipse. If the whole face of the sun is obscured, then it is a total eclipse. The darkest shadow of the moon is the **umbra**, while the lighter one is the **penumbra**.

MATERIALS: globe, flashlight or slide/filmstrip projector, orange or tennis ball

- Darken your classroom. Have one of your students stand a foot or two from the wall. Shine a light at the student and have the class notice the shadow of the student projected on the wall. The shadow goes from light (penumbra) to dark (umbra).

- Darken your classroom. Shine the light source (sun) from five feet away on the globe (earth). Place the orange (moon) between the sun and the earth. Have your students look at the globe from a position behind the light source. A shadow will appear on the globe.

- Place the observers behind the globe and block all the light with orange. This will simulate a total eclipse.

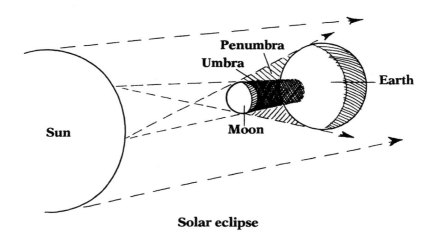

Solar eclipse

69. ECLIPSE OF THE MOON

A lunar eclipse occurs when the earth comes between the sun and the moon. The moon darkens as it moves into the earth's shadow. The darkest earth shadow is the umbra, the lighter one the penumbra.

MATERIALS: globe, flashlight or slide/filmstrip projector, orange or tennis ball

- Darken your classroom. Shine the light source (sun) from five feet away on the globe (earth). Place the orange (moon) in the shadow behind the globe. Have your students look at the orange from a position beside the globe. They will observe that the orange is in the globe's shadow.

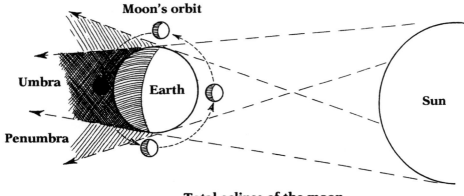

Total eclipse of the moon

70. INERTIA

The word *inertia* means "laziness" in Latin. Objects at rest want to stay at rest and objects in motion want to continue to move. That is true until another force acts on them. This is also Newton's first law. Objects in motion usually slow down since friction force opposes motion. Planets stay in orbit and stellar mechanics are orderly due to the law of inertia.

MATERIALS: index card, coin, broom, large jar (plastic if possible), some cloth, billiard ball, pie tin, plastic cup, table

- Balance an index card horizontally on one of your fingers. Place a coin on top of it. Remove the card by flicking its edge with your finger. Practice this until the coin remains on your finger.

- Place a billiard ball on top of an inverted cup, sitting in the middle of a pie tin, on top of a jar. Center the entire assembly. Then place it near the edge of a table, so that the jar is near the table's edge while the pie tin goes beyond the table's edge. Hold the broom vertically so that it touches the table's edge. Step on the bottom of the broom. Pull the handle away from the table and let go. With practice, the broom will hit the pie tin (the table's edge will stop the travel of the broom), and the ball will fall into the jar.

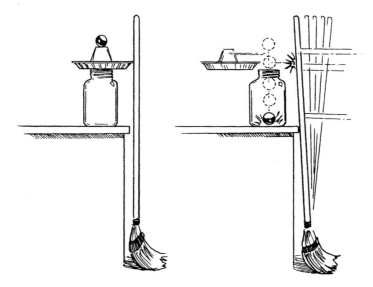

CAUTION! If you use a glass jar, place a rag or some packaging material inside it to prevent the falling ball from shattering it.

71. GRAVITATIONAL ATTRACTION

The force of **gravity** pulls all objects down. If you throw an object, it goes forward and down. Earth is not the only thing that pulls or has the force of gravity. All stars and planets in the universe have gravity. The force of gravitational attraction keeps planets in orbit around the stars.

MATERIALS: piece of string, roll of masking tape

- Drop any object. This demonstrates earth's gravity.

- Tie the roll of tape to the end of the string and start spinning it around. It will go in a circular path. The string represents the invisible force of gravity that keeps planets in orbit. If you let go, it will continue going forward and finally it will land on the floor. This shows the gravitational pull of the earth on the roll.

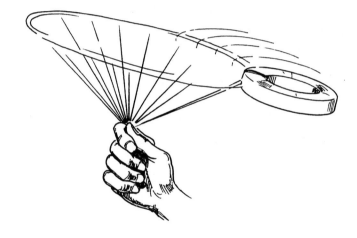

72. DRAWING A PLANET'S ORBIT

Earth and the other planets travel in elliptical orbits around the sun. Ellipses are ovals. **Aphelion** is the point at which a planet is farthest (B) from the sun. **Perihelion** is the point at which a planet is closest to the sun (A). A planet's motion around the sun is a **revolution**. Earth's revolution takes a year to complete.

MATERIALS: string, two pins, pencil, sheet of paper, sheet of cardboard

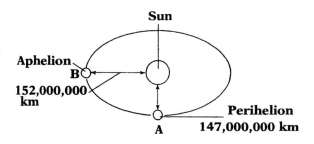

- Cut a piece of string about 30 centimeters long. Tie the ends together to make a loop. Place the paper on top of the cardboard. Draw a centerline parallel to the longer side of the sheet of paper. Stick the two pins into the centerline, approximately one-third of the way from each end of the paper. While someone holds the pins, place the string loop over the pins and draw an ellipse by keeping the pencil taut inside the string loop.

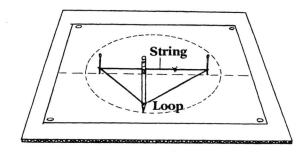

73. EARTH'S ROTATION: DAY AND NIGHT

The earth turns on its axis once a day. The side of the planet facing the sun has daylight, while the opposite side has night. This motion of the earth is **rotation**. The earth rotates on an axis that is 23.5° off the vertical. This accounts for the difference in the length of the days and nights between summer and winter.

MATERIALS: globe, flashlight

- Darken the room. Shine the light on one side of the globe from about five feet away. Have the students observe from one of the sides of the globe. Gently turn the globe from west to east to simulate earth's rotation.

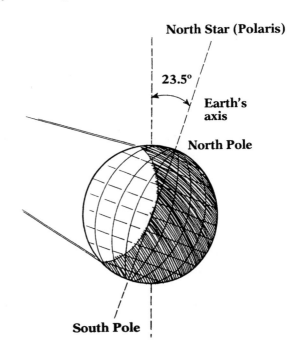

74. THE POLES ARE COLDER THAN THE EQUATOR

The polar regions are colder than the equatorial regions because at the poles the rays of the sun come at a slant. At the equator, the rays of the sun shine nearly perpendicularly to the earth's surface. By being perpendicular, the rays carry more energy, because the energy is concentrated over a smaller surface area. At the poles, the same energy is distributed over larger areas, and therefore very little is available per square unit as compared to the equator.

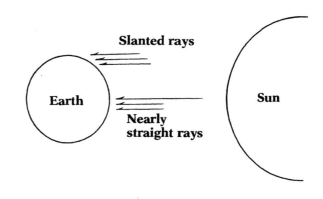

MATERIALS: flashlight or slide/filmstrip projector

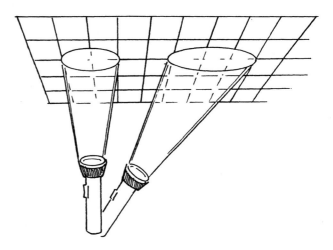

• Darken the classroom and aim the flashlight at the ceiling. First show the small area lit up by a beam perpendicular to the ceiling. Start slanting the light until the beam covers a large ceiling area. If you have ceiling tiles, count them at the start and at the end. Point out to your students that you have not changed the light source; therefore, there must be less light energy per square area illuminated, since the same light is spread out over a much larger area. The same is true for the sun's rays.

75. Seasons

Prerequisite: Demonstration 74, Poles Are Colder Than the Equator. Seasons change due to the earth's rotation around the sun. Since earth is slanted by 23.5° of the vertical, for six months the Northern Hemisphere receives straight rays of the sun while the Southern Hemisphere receives slanted rays. At this time it is summer in the Northern Hemisphere and winter in the Southern. Six months later, the situation is reversed.

MATERIALS: two plastic glasses or cups, orange or other spherical object, felt pen, two toothpicks, masking tape, flashlight or projector

- Follow these steps:

1. Prepare the orange by sticking the two toothpicks into its opposite sides. Allow about two inches of each toothpick to stick out, to represent the earth's axis. Mark a great circle on the orange, to mark its equator. Place the orange on a glass with the axis offset from perpendicular (straight up and down) by 20 to 30°.

2. Using a table or the floor, place the flashlight horizontally on the glass and tape it down, to prevent its rolling off. Turn on the flashlight. Place the model of the earth (the orange on the glass) 30 to 40 inches from the flashlight. Make certain that its axis is pointing away from the light. Have students notice that the Southern Hemisphere receives light that is almost perpendicular, while the Northern Hemisphere receives light that is slanted. This shows winter in the Northern Hemisphere, where there is less solar energy per square meter or yard. It is summer in the Southern Hemisphere.

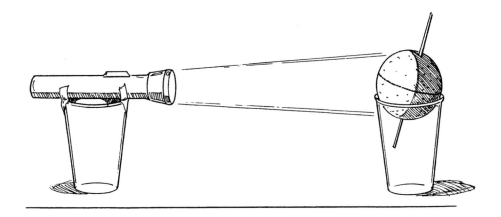

3. Move the cup 90° to the light, but be careful not to turn the cup, so its axis will remain pointed as in step 2. Maintain the same distance. Turn on the flashlight and notice that the light equally covers both hemispheres. This is true because neither hemisphere is slanted at this point. This represents spring and fall.

4. Again move the cup 90°. Be careful not to change the direction of the axis. Now the Northern Hemisphere receives light that is almost perpendicular, while the Southern Hemisphere receives light at a slant. It is summer in the Northern Hemisphere and winter in the southern one. The next 90° position will again be fall and spring.

5. Point out that the Northern Hemisphere has winter when earth is closer to the sun in its elliptical orbit. Therefore it is not the distance, but the angle of the earth to the sun, that determines the seasons.

Appendix

ASTRONOMICAL DATA #1

	Units	Sun	Mercury	Venus	Earth	Moon	Mars	Jupiter	Saturn	Uranus	Neptune	Pluto
Average distance from the sun	Miles (in millions)	25 trillion to nearest star	36	67.2	92.9	238,900 from earth	141.6	483.3	886.7	1,782	2,794	5,900
Average distance from the sun	Kilometers (in millions)	41 trillion to nearest star	57.9	108.1	149.5	384,500 from earth	227.8	778.3	1,427	2,869	4,497	5,900
Average distance from the sun	Astronomical units	4.3 light-years to nearest star	0.387	0.723	1.00	0.0026 from earth	1.524	5.203	9.539	19.18	30.06	39.44
Length of year (siderial)	Period of orbit	246 million years to orbit galaxy	88.0 days	224.7 days	365.26 days	27.32 days to orbit earth	1.88 years	11.86 years	29.46 years	84.01 years	164.8 years	247.7 years
Length of day	Period of rotation	25d8h24m equatorial	58d16h2m	243d0h14m retrograde	23h56m4s	27d7h43m	24h37m12s	9h48m48s equatorial	10h39m24s equatorial	15h36m? retrograde	18h30m?	6d9h23m
Orbital speed average	Miles per hour average	560,000 around galactic ctr.	107,300	78,500	66,800	2,300	54,100	29,300	21,600	15,300	12,200	10,600
Orbital speed average	Kilometers per hour average	900,000 around galactic ctr.	172,700	126,300	107,400	5,700	87,000	47,200	34,800	24,500	19,600	17,100
Equatorial diameter	Miles	865,000	3,031	7,521	7,927	2,160	4,197	88,733	74,600	31,600	30,200	1,900?
Equatorial diameter	Kilometers	1,392,000	4,878	12,104	12,756	3,476	6,794	142,796	120,000	50,800	48,600	3,000?
Equatorial diameter	Earth = 1	109	0.382	0.949	1.00	0.2725	0.5326	11.19	9.41	3.98	3.81	0.24?
Mass	Earth = 1	332,946	0.055	0.815	1.00	0.012	0.107	317.9	95.17	14.56	17.24	0.002?
Volume	Earth = 1	1,300,000	0.056	0.855	1.00	0.020	0.151	1,403	833	63.0	55.3	0.013?
Density mean	g/cm³ Water = 1	1.41	5.44	5.24	5.52	3.36	3.93	1.33	0.70	1.28	1.75	0.69?
Gravity on surface	Earth = 1	27.8	0.38	0.90	1.00	0.16	0.38	2.87	1.32	0.93	1.23	0.03?

Legend: d = days   h = hours   m = minutes   s = seconds   ? = approximate

ASTRONOMICAL DATA #2

	Units	Sun	Mercury	Venus	Earth	Moon	Mars	Jupiter	Saturn	Uranus	Neptune	Pluto
Escape velocity	Miles per hour	1,378,000	9,619	23,042	25,055	5,324	11,185	141,828	88,139	48,096	54,136	751?
Escape velocity	Kilometers per second	616	4.3	10.3	11.2	2.3	5.0	63.4	39.4	21.5	24.2	0.34?
Temperature extremes	High core Fahrenheit	27,000,000 °F	660°F	896°F	136.4°F	225°F	80°F	53,500°F				−390°F
Temperature extremes	High core Celsius	15,000,000 °C	350°C	480°C	58°C	107°C	27°C	29,700°C				−234°C
Temperature extremes	Low core Fahrenheit	10,800°F	−270°F	−27°F†	−126.9°F	−243°F	−190°F	−140°F†	−292°F†	−346°F†	−364°F†	−382°F?
Temperature extremes	Low core Celsius	6,000°C	−170°C	−33°C†	−88.3°C	−153°C	−123°C	−95°C†	−180°C†	−210°C†	−220°C†	−230°C?
Number of known moons		9 Planets	0	0	1	—	2	16+ rings	23? rings	5+ rings	2	1
Eccentricity in orbit	Circular orbit = 0	—	0.206	0.007	0.017	0.055	0.093	0.048	0.056	0.047	0.009	0.250
Inclination of equator	To orbital plane of planets	7.25° Equator to ecliptic	<2°	183.4°	23.45°	6.7°	23.98°	3.1°	26.7°	97.9°	28.8°	90°?
Oblateness of planet		0	0	0	0.003	0.0005	0.009	0.063	0.109	0.063	0.026	?
Atmosphere	Principal gases	H_2, He	none	CO_2	N_2, O_2	none	CO_2	H_2, He	H_2, He	H_2, He	H_2, He	none

Legend: † = cloudtops   ? = approximate CO_2 = carbon dioxide N_2 = nitrogen H_2 = hydrogen   He = Helium

MOONS IN THE SOLAR SYSTEM

The moons are arranged in their order of closeness from the planets.

Earth	Mars	Jupiter	Saturn	Uranus	Neptune	Pluto
1. Moon	1. Phobos	1. 1979-J3	1. 1980-S28	1. Miranda	1. Triton	1. Charon
	2. Deimos	2. Adrastea	2. 1980-S27	2. Ariel	2. Nereid	
		3. Amalthea	3. 1980-S26	3. Ubrial		
		4. 1972-J2	4. 1980-S1	4. Titania		
		5. Io	5. 1980-S3	5. Oberon		
		6. Europa	6. Mimas			
		7. Ganymede	7. Enceladus			
		8. Callisto	8. Tethys			
		9. Leda	9. Tethys B			
		10. Himalia	10. Tethys C			
		11. Lysithea	11. Dione			
		12. Elara	12. Dione B			
		13. Ananke	13. Rhea			
		14. Carme	14. Titan			
		15. Pasiphae	15. Hyperion			
		16. Sinope	16. Iapetus			
			17. Phoebe			
			At least six more are suspected to be there.			

DENSITY OF LIQUIDS

	approx. gm/cm^3 at 20°C
Acetone	0.79
Alcohol (ethyl)	0.79
Alcohol (methyl)	0.81
Benzene	0.90
Carbon disulfide	1.29
Carbon tetrachloride	1.56
Chloroform	1.50
Ether	0.74
Gasoline	0.68
Glycerin	1.26
Kerosene	0.82
Linseed oil (boiled)	0.94
Mercury	13.6
Milk	1.03
Naphtha (petroleum)	0.67
Olive oil	0.92
Sulfuric acid	1.82
Turpentine	0.87
Water0^o C	0.99
Water4^o C	1.00
Water - sea	1.03

ALTITUDE, BAROMETER, AND BOILING POINT

altitude (approx. ft)	barometer reading(cm of mercury)	boiling point (^{o} C)
15,430	43.1	84.9
10,320	52.0	89.8
6190	60.5	93.8
5510	62.0	94.4
5060	63.1	94.9
4500	64.4	95.4
3950	65.7	96.0
3500	66.8	96.4
3060	67.9	96.9
2400	69.6	97.6
2060	70.4	97.9
1520	71.8	98.5
970	73.3	99.0
530	74.5	99.5
0	76.0	100.0
- 550	77.5	100.5

SPECIFIC GRAVITY

gram /cm^3 at 20° C.

Agate	2.5-2.6	Granite*	2.7	Polystyrene	1.06
Aluminum	2.7	Graphite	2.2	Quartz	2.6
Brass*	8.5	Human body - normal	1.07	Rock salt	2.1-2.2
Butter	0.86	Human body - lungs full	1.00	Rubber (gum)	0.92
Cellural cellulose acetate	0.75	Ice	0.92	Silver	10.5
Celluloid	1.4	Iron (cast)*	7.9	Steel	7.8
Cement*	2.8	Lead	11.3	Sulfur (roll)	2.0
Coal (anthracite)*	1.5	Limestone	2.7	Tin	7.3
Coal (bituminous)*	1.3	Magnesium	1.74	Tungsten	18.8
Copper	8.9	Marble*	2.7	Wood Rock Elm	0.76
Cork	0.22-0.26	Nickel	8.8	Balsa	0.16
Diamond	3.1-3.5	Opal	2.1-2.3	Red Oak	0.67
German Silver	8.4	Osmium	22.5	Southern Pine	0.56
Glass (common)	2.5	Paraffin	0.9	White Pine	0.4
Gold	19.3	Platinum	21.4	Zinc	7.1

*Non homogeneous material. Specific gravity may vary. Table gives average value.

CONVERSIONS OF TEMPERATURE CELSIUS–FAHRENHEIT

C°	F°	C°	F°	C°	F°	C°	F°	C°	F°	C°	F°
250	482.00	200	392.00	150	302.00	100	212.00	50	122.00	0	32.00
249	480.20	199	390.20	149	300.20	99	210.20	49	120.20	-1	30.20
248	478.40	198	388.40	148	298.40	98	208.40	48	118.40	-2	28.40
247	476.60	197	386.60	147	296.60	97	206.60	47	116.60	-3	26.60
246	474.80	196	384.80	146	294.80	96	204.80	46	114.80	-4	24.80
245	473.00	195	383.00	145	293.00	95	203.00	45	113.00	-5	23.00
244	471.20	194	381.20	144	291.20	94	201.20	44	111.20	-6	21.20
243	469.40	193	379.40	143	289.40	93	199.40	43	109.40	-7	19.40
242	467.60	192	377.60	142	287.60	92	197.60	42	107.60	-8	17.60
241	465.80	191	375.80	141	285.80	91	195.80	41	105.80	-9	15.80
240	464.00	190	374.00	140	284.00	90	194.00	40	104.00	-10	14.00
239	462.20	189	372.20	139	282.20	89	192.20	39	102.20	-11	12.20
238	460.40	188	370.40	138	280.40	88	190.40	38	100.40	-12	10.40
237	458.60	187	368.60	137	278.60	87	188.60	37	98.60	-13	8.60
236	456.80	186	366.80	136	276.80	86	186.80	36	96.80	-14	6.80
235	455.00	185	365.00	135	275.00	85	185.00	35	95.00	-15	5.00
234	453.20	184	363.20	134	273.20	84	183.20	34	93.20	-16	3.20
233	451.40	183	361.40	133	271.40	83	181.40	33	91.40	-17	1.40
232	449.60	182	359.60	132	269.60	82	179.60	32	89.60	-18	-0.40
231	447.80	181	357.80	131	267.80	81	177.80	31	87.80	-19	-2.20
230	446.00	180	356.00	130	266.00	80	176.00	30	86.00	-20	-4.00
229	444.20	179	354.20	129	264.20	79	174.20	29	84.20	-21	-5.80
228	442.40	178	352.40	128	262.40	78	172.40	28	82.40	-22	-7.60
227	440.60	177	350.60	127	260.60	77	170.60	27	80.60	-23	-9.40
226	438.80	176	348.80	126	258.80	76	168.80	26	78.80	-24	-11.20
225	437.00	175	347.00	125	257.00	75	167.00	25	77.00	-25	-13.00
224	435.20	174	345.20	124	255.20	74	165.20	24	75.20	-26	-14.80
223	433.40	173	343.40	123	253.40	73	163.40	23	73.40	-27	-16.60
222	431.60	172	341.60	122	251.60	72	161.60	22	71.60	-28	-18.40
221	429.80	171	339.80	121	249.80	71	159.80	21	69.80	-29	-20.20
220	428.00	170	338.00	120	248.00	70	158.00	20	68.00	-30	-22.00
219	426.20	169	336.20	119	246.20	69	156.20	19	66.20	-31	-23.80
218	424.40	168	334.40	118	244.40	68	154.40	18	64.40	-32	-25.60
217	422.60	167	332.60	117	242.60	67	152.60	17	62.60	-33	-27.40
216	420.80	166	330.80	116	240.80	66	150.80	16	60.80	-34	-29.20
215	419.00	165	329.00	115	239.00	65	149.00	15	59.00	-35	-31.00
214	417.20	164	327.20	114	237.20	64	147.20	14	57.20	-36	-32.80
213	415.40	163	325.40	113	235.40	63	145.40	13	55.40	-37	-34.60
212	413.60	162	323.60	112	233.60	62	143.60	12	53.60	-38	-36.40
211	411.80	161	321.80	111	231.80	61	141.80	11	51 80	-39	-38 20
210	410.00	160	320.00	110	230.00	60	140.00	10	50.00	-40	-40 00
209	408.20	159	318.20	109	228.20	59	138.20	9	48.20	-41	-41.80
208	406.40	158	316.40	108	226.40	58	136.40	8	46.40	-42	-43.60
207	404.60	157	314.60	107	224.60	57	134.60	7	44.60	-43	-45.40
206	402.80	156	312.80	106	222.80	56	132.80	6	42.80	-44	-47.20
205	401.00	155	311.00	105	221.00	55	131.00	5	41.00	-45	-49.00
204	399.20	154	309.20	104	219.20	54	129.20	4	39.20	-46	-50.80
203	397.40	153	307.40	103	217.40	53	127.40	3	37.40	-47	-52.60
202	395.60	152	305.60	102	215.60	52	125.60	2	35.60	-48	-54.40
201	393.80	151	303.80	101	213.80	51	123.80	1	33.80	-49	-56.20

CONVERSIONS OF TEMPERATURE FAHRENHEIT–CELSIUS

F°	C°	F°	C°	F°	C°	F°	C°	F°	C°	F°	C°
250	121.11	200	93.33	150	65.56	100	37.78	50	10.00	0	-17.78
249	120.56	199	92.78	149	65.00	99	37.22	49	9.44	-1	-18.33
248	120.00	198	92.22	148	64.44	98	36.67	48	8.89	-2	-18.89
247	119.44	197	91.67	147	63.89	97	36.11	47	8.33	-3	-19.44
246	118.89	196	91.11	146	63.33	96	35.56	46	7.78	-4	-20.00
245	118.33	195	90.56	145	62.78	95	35.00	45	7.22	-5	-20.56
244	117.78	194	90.00	144	62.22	94	34.44	44	6.67	-6	-21.11
243	117.22	193	89.44	143	61.67	93	33.89	43	6.11	-7	-21.67
242	116.67	192	88.89	142	61.11	92	33.33	42	5.56	-8	-22.22
241	116.11	191	88.33	141	60.56	91	32.78	41	5.00	-9	-22.78
240	115.56	190	87.78	140	60.00	90	32.22	40	4.44	-10	-23.33
239	115.00	189	87.22	139	59.44	89	31.67	39	3.89	-11	-23.89
238	114.44	188	86.67	138	58.89	88	31.11	38	3.33	-12	-24.44
237	113.89	187	86.11	137	58.33	87	30.56	37	2.78	-13	-25.00
236	113.33	186	85.56	136	57.78	86	30.00	36	2.22	-14	-25.56
235	112.78	185	85.00	135	57.22	85	29.44	35	1.67	-15	-26.11
234	112.22	184	84.44	134	56.67	84	28.89	34	1.11	-16	-26.67
233	111.67	183	83.89	133	56.11	83	28.33	33	0.56	-17	-27.22
232	111.11	182	83.33	132	55.56	82	27.78	32	0.00	-18	-27.78
231	110.56	181	82.78	131	55.00	81	27.22	31	-0.56	-19	-28.33
230	110.00	180	82.22	130	54.44	80	26.67	30	-1.11	-20	-28.89
229	109.44	179	81.67	129	53.89	79	26.11	29	-1.67	-21	-29.44
228	108.89	178	81.11	128	53.33	78	25.56	28	-2.22	-22	-30.00
227	108.33	177	80.56	127	52.78	77	25.00	27	-2.78	-23	-30.56
226	107.78	176	80.00	126	52.22	76	24.44	26	-3.33	-24	-31.11
225	107.22	175	79.44	125	51.67	75	23.89	25	-3.89	-25	-31.67
224	106.67	174	78.89	124	51.11	74	23.33	24	-4.44	-26	-32.22
223	106.11	173	78.33	123	50.56	73	22.78	23	-5.00	-27	-32.78
222	105.56	172	77.78	122	50.00	72	22.22	22	-5.56	-28	-33.33
221	105.00	171	77.22	121	49.44	71	21.67	21	-6.11	-29	-33.89
220	104.44	170	76.67	120	48.89	70	21.11	20	-6.67	-30	-34.44
219	103.89	169	76.11	119	48.33	69	20.56	19	-7.22	-31	-35.00
218	103.33	168	75.56	118	47.78	68	20.00	18	-7.78	-32	-35.56
217	102.78	167	75.00	117	47.22	67	19.44	17	-8.33	-33	-36.11
216	102.22	166	74.44	116	46.67	66	18.89	16	-8.89	-34	-36.67
215	101.67	165	73.89	115	46.11	65	18.33	15	-9.44	-35	-37.22
214	101.11	164	73.33	114	45.56	64	17.78	14	-10.00	-36	-37.78
213	100.56	163	72.78	113	45.00	63	17.22	13	-10.56	-37	-38.33
212	100.00	162	72.22	112	44.44	62	16.67	12	-11.11	-38	-38.89
211	99.44	161	71.67	111	43.89	61	16.11	11	-11.67	-39	-39.44
210	98.89	160	71.11	110	43.33	60	15.56	10	-12.22	-40	-40.00
209	98.33	159	70.56	109	42.78	59	15.00	9	-12.78	-41	-40.56
208	97.78	158	70.00	108	42.22	58	14.44	8	-13.33	-42	-41.11
207	97.22	157	69.44	107	41.67	57	13.89	7	-13.89	-43	-41.67
206	96.67	156	68.89	106	41.11	56	13.33	6	-14.44	-44	-42.22
205	96.11	155	68.33	105	40.56	55	12.78	5	-15.00	-45	-42.78
204	95.56	154	67.78	104	40.00	54	12.22	4	-15.56	-46	-43.33
203	95.00	153	67.22	103	39.44	53	11.67	3	-16.11	-47	-43.89
202	94.44	152	66.67	102	38.89	52	11.11	2	-16.67	-48	-44.44
201	93.89	151	66.11	101	38.33	51	10.56	1	-17.22	-49	-45.00

UNITS CONVERSIONS AND CONSTANTS

FROM	TO	X BY
Acres	Square feet	43560
Acres	Square meters	4046.8564
Acre-feet	Cu-feet	43560
Avogadro's number	6.02252×10^{23}	
Barrel (US dry)	Barrel (US liquid)	0.96969
Barrel (US liq.)	Barrel (US dry)	1.03125
Bars	Atmospheres	0.98692
Bars	Grams/sq.cm.	1019.716
Cubic feet	Acre-feet	2.2956841×10^{-5}
Cubic feet	Cu.centimeters	28316.847
Cubic feet	Cu.meters	0.028316984
Cubic feet	Gallons (US liquid)	7.4805195
Cubic feet	Quarts (US liquid)	29.922078
Cubic inches	Cu. centimeters	16.38706
Cubic inches	Cu. feet	0.0005787037
Cubic inches	Gallons (US liquid)	0.004329004
Cubic inches	Liters	0.016387064
Cubic inches	Ounces (US, fluid)	0.5541125
Cubic inches	Quarts (US. liquid)	0.03463203
Cubic meters	Acre-feet	0.0008107131
Cubic meters	Barrels (US liquid)	8.386414
Cubic meters	Cubic feet	35.314667
Cubic meters	Gallons (US liquid)	264.17205
Cubic meters	Quarts (US Liquid)	1056.6882
Cu. yards	Cu. Cm.	764554.86
Cu. yards	Cu. feet	27
Cu. yards	Cu. inches	46,656
Cu. yards	Liters	764.55486
Cu. yards	Quarts (US Liquid)	807.89610
Days (mean solar)	Days (Sidereal)	1.0027379
Days (mean solar)	Hours (mean solar)	24
Days (mean solar)	Hours (sidereal)	24.065710
Days (mean solar)	Years (Calendar)	0.002739726
Days (mean solar)	Years (sidereal)	0.0027378031
Days (mean solar)	Years (tropical)	0.0027379093
Days (sidereal)	Days (mean solar)	0.99726957
Days (sidereal)	Hours (mean solar)	23.93447
Days (sidereal)	Hours (sidereal)	24
Days (sidereal)	Minutes (mean solar)	1436.0682
Days (sidereal)	Minutes (sidereal)	1440
Days (sidereal)	Second (sidereal)	86400
Days (sidereal)	Years (calendar)	0.0027322454
Days (sidereal)	Years (sidereal)	0.0027303277

UNITS: CONVERSIONS AND CONSTANTS *(continued)*

FROM	TO	X BY
Days (sidereal)	Years (tropical)	0.0027304336
Decibels	Bels	0.1
Decimeters	Feet	0.32808399
Decimeters	Inches	3.9370079
Degrees	Minutes	60
Degrees	Radians	0.017453293
Degrees	Seconds	3600
Dekameters	Feet	32.808399
Dekameters	Inches	393.70079
Dekameters	Yards	10.93613
Decimeters	Feet	0.32808399
Decimeters	Inches	3.9370079
Decimeters	Meters	0.1
Degrees	Circles	0.0027777
Degrees	Minutes	60
Degrees	Quadrants	0.0111111
Degrees	Radians	0.017453293
Degrees	Seconds ,	600
Dekaliters	Pecks (U.S.)	1.135136
Dekameters	Pints (U.S. dry)	19.16217
Dekameters	Centimeters	1000
Dekameters	Feet	32.808399
Dekameters	Inches	393.70079
Dekameters	Yards	10.93613
Fathoms	Centimeters	182.88
Fathoms	Feet	6
Fathoms	Inches	72
Fathoms	Meters	1.8288
Fathoms	Miles (naut. Int.)	0.00098747300
Fathoms	Miles (statute)	0.001136363
Fathoms	Yards	2
Feet	Centimeters	30.48
Feet	Fathoms	0.166666
Feet	Furlongs	0.00151515
Feet	Inches	12
Feet	Meters	0.3048
Feet	Microns	304800
Feet	Miles (naut. Int.)	0.00016457883
Feet	Miles (statute)	0.000189393
Feet	Rods	0.060606
Feet	Yards	0.333333
Gallons (U.S. liq.).	Acre-feet	3.0688833×10^{-6}

UNITS: CONVERSIONS AND CONSTANTS *(continued)*

FROM	TO	X BY
Gallons (U.S. liq.)	Barrels (U.S. liq.)	0.031746032
Gallons (U.S. liq.)	Bushels (U.S.)	0.10742088
Gallons (U.S. liq.)	Cu. centimeters	3785.4118
Gallons (U.S. liq.)	Cu. feet	0.133680555
Gallons (U.S. liq.)	Cu.inches	231
Gallons (U.S. liq.)	Cu. meters	0.0037854118
Gallons (U.S. liq.)	Cu. yards	0.0049511317
Gallons (U.S. liq.)	Gallons (U.S. dry)	0.85936701
Gallons (U.S. liq.)	Gallons (wine)	1
Gallons (U.S. liq.)	Gills (U.S.)	32
Gallons (U.S. liq.)	Liters	3.7854118
Gallons (U.S. liq.)	Ounces (U.S. fluid)	128
Gallons (U.S. liq.)	Pints (U.S. liq.)	8
Gallons (U.S. liq.)	Quarts (U.S. liq.)	4
Grains	Carats (metric)	0.32399455
Grains	Drams (apoth. or troy)	0.016666
Grains	Drams (avdp.)	0.036671429
Grains	Grams	0.06479891
Grains	Milligrams	64.79891
Grains	Ounces (apoth. or troy)	0.0020833
Grains	Ounces (avdp.)	0.0022857143
Grams	Carats (metric)	5
Grams	Drams (apoth. or troy)	0.25720597
Grams	Drams (avdp.)	0.56438339
Grams	Dynes	980.665
Grams	Grains	15.432358
Grams	Ounces (apoth. or troy)	0.032150737
Grams	Ounces (avdp.)	0.035273962
Gravitational constant	Cm./(sec. X sec.)	980.621
Gravitational constant = G	dyne cm^2 g^{-2}	6.6732(31) X 10^{-8}
Gravitational constant	Ft./(sec. X sec.)	32.1725
Gravitational constant = G	N m^2 kg^{-2}	6.6732(31) X 10^{-11}
Gravity on Earth =1	Gravity on Jupiter	2.305
Gravity on Earth =1	Gravity on Mars	0.3627 Equatorial
Gravity on Earth =1	Gravity on Mercury	0.3648 Equatorial
Gravity on Earth =1	Gravity on Moon	0.1652 Equatorial
Gravity on Earth =1	Gravity on Neptune	1.323 ± 0.210 Equatorial
Gravity on Earth =1	Gravity on Pluto	0.0225 ± 0.217 Equatorial
Gravity on Earth =1	Gravity on Saturn	0.8800 Equatorial
Gravity on Earth =1	Gravity on Sun	27.905 Equatorial
Gravity on Earth =1	Gravity on Uranus	0.9554 ± 0.168

Units: Conversions and Constants *(continued)*

FROM	TO	X BY
		Equatorial
Gravity on Earth =1	Gravity on Venus	0.9049 Equatorial
Hectares	Acres	2.4710538
Hectares	Sq. feet	107639.10
Hectares	Sq. meters	10000
Hectares	Sq. miles	0.0038610216
Hectares	Sq. rods	395.36861
Hectograms	Pounds (apoth or troy)	0.26792289
Hectograms	Pounds (avdp.)	0.22046226
Hectoliters	Cu. cm.	1.00028×10^5
Hectoliters	Cu. feet	3.531566
Hectoliters	Gallons (U.S. liq.)	26.41794
Hectoliters	Ounces (U.S.) fluid	3381.497
Hectoliters	Pecks (U.S.)	11.35136
Hectometers	Feet	328.08399
Hectometers	Rods	19.883878
Hectometers	Yards	109.3613
Horsepower	Horsepower (electric)	0.999598
Horsepower	Horsepower (metric)	1.01387
Horsepower	Kilowatts	0.745700
Horsepower	Kilowatts (Int.)	0.745577
Horsepower-hours	Kw.-hours	0.745700
Horsepower-hours	Watt-hours	745.700
Hours (mean solar)	Days (mean solar)	0.0416666
Hours (mean solar)	Days (sidereal)	0.041780746
Hours (mean solar)	Hours (sidereal)	1.00273791
Hours (mean solar)	Minutes (mean solar)	60
Hours (mean solar)	Minutes (sidereal)	60.164275
Hours (mean solar)	Seconds (mean solar)	3600
Hours (mean solar)	Seconds (sidereal)	3609.8565
Hours (mean solar)	Weeks (mean calendar)	0.0059523809
Hours (sidereal)	Days (mean solar)	0.41552899
Hours (sidereal)	Days (sidereal)	0.0416666
Hours (sidereal)	Hours (mean solar)	0.99726957
Hours (sidereal)	Minutes (mean solar)	59.836174
Hours (sidereal)	Minutes (sidereal)	60
Inches	Ångström units	2.54×10^8
Inches	Centimeters	2.54
Inches	Cubits	0.055555
Inches	Fathoms	0.013888
Inches	Feet	0.083333
Inches	Meters	0.0254

UNITS: CONVERSIONS AND CONSTANTS *(continued)*

FROM	TO	X BY
Inches	Mils	1000
Inches	Yards	0.027777
Kilograms	Drams(apoth. or troy)	257.20597
Kilograms	Drams (avdp.)	564.38339
Kilograms	Dynes	980665
Kilograms	Grains	15432.358
Kilograms	Hundredweights (long)	0.019684131
Kilograms	Hundredweights (short)	0.022046226
Kilograms	Ounces (apoth. or troy)	32.150737
Kilograms	Ounces (avdp.)	35.273962
Kilograms	Pennyweights	643.01493
Kilograms	Pounds (apoth. or troy)	2.6792289
Kilograms	Pounds (avdp.)	2.2046226
Kilograms	Quarters (U.S. long)	0.0039368261
Kilograms	Scruples (apoth.)	771.61792
Kilograms	Tons (long)	0.00098420653
Kilograms	Tons (metric)	0.001
Kilograms	Tons (short)	0.0011023113
Kilograms/cu. meter	Grams/cu. cm.	0.001
Kilograms/cu. meter	Lb. /cu. ft.	0.062427961
Kilograms/cu. meter	Lb./cu. inch	3.6127292×10^{-5}
Kiloliters	Cu. centimeters	1×10^{6}
Kiloliters	Cu. feet	35.31566
Kiloliters	Cu. inches	61025.45
Kiloliters	Cu. meters	1.000028
Kiloliters	Cu. yards	1.307987
Kiloliters	Gallons (U.S. dry)	27.0271
Kiloliters	Gallons (U.S. liq.)	264.1794
Kilometers	Astronomical units	6.68878×10^{-9}
Kilometers	Feet	3280.8399
Kilometers	Light years	1.05702×10^{-13}
Kilometers	Miles (naut. Int.)	0.53995680
Kilometers	Miles (statute)	0.62137119
Kilometers	Rods	198.83878
Kilometers	Yards	1093.6133
Kilometers/hr.	Cm./sec.	27.7777
Kilometers/hr.	Feet/hr.	3280.8399
Kilometers/hr.	Feet/min.	54.680665
Kilometers/hr.	Knots (Int.)	0.53995680
Kilometers/hr.	Meters/sec.	0.277777
Kilometers/hr.	Miles (statute)/hr.	0.62137119
Kilometers/min.	Cm./sec.	1666.666

UNITS: CONVERSIONS AND CONSTANTS *(continued)*

FROM	TO	X BY
Kilometers/min.	Feet/min.	3280.8399
Kilometers/min.	Kilometers/hr.	60
Kilometers/min.	Knots (Int.)	32.397408
Kilometers/min.	Miles/hr.	37.282272
Kilometers/min.	Miles/min.	0.62137119
Kilowatt-hours	Joules	3.6×10^6
Light, velocity of	299,792.4562 Km/sec. ± 1.1	meter/sec. (100x more accurate)
Light, velocity of	m/sec. ± 0.33ppm	$2.9979250(10) \times 10^8$
Light, velocity of	cm/sec. ± 0.33ppm	$2.9979250(10) \times 10^{10}$
Light years	Astronomical units	63279.5
Light years	Kilometers	9.46055×10^{12}
Light years	Miles (statute)	5.87851×10^{12}
Liters	Bushels (U.S.)	0.02837839
Liters	Cu. centimeters	1000
Liters	Cu. feet	0.03531566
Liters	Cu. inches	61.02545
Liters	Cu. meters	0.001
Liters	Cu. yards	0.001307987
Liters	Drams (U.S. fluid)	270.5198
Liters	Gallons (U.S. dry)	0.2270271
Liters	Gallons (U.S. liq.)	0.2641794
Liters	Gills (U.S.)	8.453742
Liters	Hogsheads	0.004193325
Liters	Minims (U.S.)	16231.19
Liters	Ounces (U.S. fluid)	33.81497
Liters	Pecks (U.S.)	0.1135136
Liters	Pints (U.S. dry)	1.816217
Liters	Pints (U.S. liq.)	2.113436
Liters	Quarts (U.S. dry)	0.9081084
Liters	Quarts (U.S. liq.)	1.056718
Liters/min	Cu. ft./min.	0.03531566
Liters/min	Cu. ft./sec.	0.0005885943
Liters/min	Gal. (U.S. liq.)/min.	0.2641794
Liters/sec.	Cu. ft./min.	2.118939
Liters/sec.	Cu. ft./sec.	0.03531566
Liters/sec.	Cu. yards/min.	0.07847923
Liters/sec.	Gal. (U.S. liq.)/min.	15.85077
Liters/sec.	Gal. (U.S. liq.)/sec.	0.2641794
Lumens	Candle power	0.079577472
Meters	Ångström units	1×10^{10}
Meters	Fathoms	0.54680665
Meters	Feet	3.2808399

UNITS: CONVERSIONS AND CONSTANTS *(continued)*

FROM	TO	X BY
Meters	Furlongs	0.0049709695
Meters	Inches	39.370079
Meters	Megameters	1×10^{-6}
Meters	Miles (naut. Int.)	0.00053995680
Meters	Miles (statute)	0.00062137119
Meters	Millimicrons	1×10^{9}
Meters	Mils	39370.079
Meters	Rods	0.19883878
Meters	Yards	1.0936133
Meters/hr.	Feet/hr.	3.2808399
Meters/hr.	Feet/min.	0.054680665
Meters/hr.	Knots (Int.)	0.00053995680
Meters/hr.	Miles (statute)/hr.	0.00062137119
Meters/min.	Cm./sec.	1.666666
Meters/min.	Feet/min.	3.2808399
Meters/min.	Feet/sec.	0.054680665
Meters/min.	Kilometers/hr.	0.06
Meters/min.	Knots (Int.)	0.032397408
Meters/min.	Miles (statute)/hr.	0.037282272
Meters/sec.	Feet/min.	196.85039
Meters/sec.	Feet/sec.	3.2808399
Meters/sec.	Kilometers/hr.	3.6
Meters/sec.	Kilometers/min.	0.06
Meters/sec.	Miles (statute)/hr.	2.2369363
Meter-candles	Lumens/sq. meter	1
Micrograms	Grams	1×10^{-6}
Micrograms	Milligrams	0.001
Micromicrons	Ångström units	0.01
Micromicrons	Centimeters	1×10^{-10}
Micromicrons	Inches	$3.9370079 \times 10^{-11}$
Micromicrons	Meters	1×10^{-12}
Micromicrons	Microns	1×10^{-6}
Microns	Ångström units	10000
Microns	Centimeters	0.0001
Microns	Feet	3.2808399×10^{-6}
Microns	Inches	3.9370070×10^{-5}
Microns	Meters	1×10^{-6}
Microns	Millimeters	0.001
Microns	Millimicrons	1000
Miles (statute)	Centimeters	160934.4
Miles (statute)	Feet	5280
Miles (statute)	Furlongs	8

UNITS: CONVERSIONS AND CONSTANTS *(continued)*

FROM	TO	X BY
Miles (statute)	Inches	63360
Miles (statute)	Kilometers	1.609344
Miles (statute)	Light years	1.70111×10^{-13}
Miles (statute)	Meters	1600.344
Miles (statute)	Miles (naut. Int.)	0.86897624
Miles (statute)	Myriameters	0.1609344
Miles (statute)	Rods	320
Miles (statute)	Yards	1760
Miles/hr.	Cm./sec.	44.704
Miles/hr.	Feet/hr.	5280
Miles/hr.	Feet/min.	88
Miles/hr.	Feet/sec	1.466666
Miles/hr.	Kilometers/hr.	1.609344
Miles/hr.	Knots (Int.)	0.86897624
Miles/hr.	Meters/min.	26.8224
Miles/hr.	Miles/min.	0.0166666
Miles/min.	Cm./sec.	2682.24
Miles/min.	Feet/hr.	316800
Miles/min.	Feet/sec.	88
Miles/min.	Kilometers/min.	1.609344
Miles/min.	Knots (Int.)	52.138574
Miles/min.	Meters/min.	1609.344
Miles/min.	Miles/hr.	60
Mlilligrams	Carats (1877)	0.004871
Mlilligrams	Carats (metric)	0.005
Mlilligrams	Drams (apoth. or troy)	0.00025720597
Mlilligrams	Drams (advp.)	0.00056438339
Milligrams	Grains	0.015432358
Milligrams	Grams	0.001
Milligrams	Ounces (apoth. or troy)	3.2150737×10^{-5}
Milligrams	Ounces (avdp.)	3.5273962×10^{-5}
Milligrams	Pounds (apoth. or troy)	2.6792289×10^{-5}
Milligrams	Pounds(avdp.)	2.2046226×10^{-6}
Milligrams/liter	Grains/gal. (U.S.)	0.05841620
Milligrams/liter	Grams/liter	0.001
Milligrams/liter	Parts/million	1; solvent density = 1
Milligrams/liter	Lb./cu. ft.	6.242621×10^{-5}
Milligrams/mm.	Dynes/cm.	9.80665
Milliliters	Cu. cm.	1
Milliliters	Cu. inches	0.06102545
Milliliters	Drams (U.S. fluid)	0.2705198
Milliliters	Gills (U.S.)	0.008453742

UNITS: CONVERSIONS AND CONSTANTS *(continued)*

FROM	TO	X BY
Milliliters	Minims (U.S.)	16.23119
Milliliters	Ounces (U.S. fluid)	0.03381497
Milliliters	Pints (U.S. liq.)	0.002113436
Millimeters	Ångatröm units	1×10^{7}
Millimeters	Centimeters	0.1
Millimeters	Decimeters	0.01
Millimeters	Dekameters	0.0001
Millimeters	Feet	0.0032808399
Millimeters	Inches	.0.039370079
Millimeters	Meters	0.001
Millimeters	Microns	1000
Millimeters	Mils	39.370079
Millimicrons	Ångström units	10
Millimicrons	Centimeters	1×10^{-7}
Millimicrons	Inches	3.9370079×10^{-8}
Millimicrons	Microns	0.001
Millimicrons	Millimeters	1×10^{-6}
Minutes (angular)	Degrees	0.0166666
Minutes (angular)	Quadrants	0.000185185
Minutes (angular)	Radians	0.00029088821
Minutes (angular)	Seconds (angular)	60
Minutes (mean solar)	Days (mean solar)	0.0006944444
Minutes (mean solar)	Days (sidereal)	0.00069634577
Minutes (mean solar)	Hours (mean solar)	0.0166666
Minutes (mean solar)	Hours (sidereal)	0.016732298
Minutes (mean solar)	Minutes (sidereal)	1.00273791
Minutes (sidereal)	Days (mean solar)	0.00069254831
Minutes (sidereal)	Minutes (mean solar)	0.99726957
Minutes (sidereal)	Months (mean calendar)	2.2768712×10^{-5}
Minutes (sidereal)	Seconds (sidereal)	60
Minutes/cm.	Radians/cm.	0.00029088821
Months (lunar)	Days (mean solar)	29.530588
Months (lunar)	Hours (mean solar)	708.73411
Months (lunar)	Minutes (mean solar)	42524.047
Months (lunar)	Second (mean solar)	2.5514428×10^{-5}
Months (lunar)	Weeks (mean calendar)	4.2186554
Months (mean calendar)	Days (mean solar)	30.416666
Months (mean calendar)	Hours (mean solar) .	730
Months (mean calendar)	Months (lunar)	1.0300055
Months (mean calendar)	Weeks (mean calendar)	4.3452381
Months (mean calendar)	Years (calendar)	0.08333333
Months (mean calendar)	Years (sidereal)	0.083274845

UNITS: CONVERSIONS AND CONSTANTS *(continued)*

FROM	TO	X BY
Months (mean calendar)	Years (tropical)	0.083278075
Myriagrams	Pounds (avdp.)	22.046226
Ounces (avdp.)	Drams (apoth. or troy)	7.291666
Ounces (avdp.)	Drams (avdp.)	16
Ounces (avdp.)	Grains	437.5
Ounces (avdp.)	Grams	28.349
Ounces (avdp.)	Ounces (apoth. or troy)	0.9114583
Ounces (avdp.)	Pounds (apoth. or troy)	0.075954861
Ounces (avdp.)	Pounds(avdp.)	0.0625
Ounces (U.S. fluid)	Cu. cm.	29.573730
Ounces (U.S. fluid)	Cu.inches	1.8046875
Ounces (U.S. fluid)	Cu. meters	2.9573730×10^{-5}
Ounces (U.S. fluid)	Drams (U.S. fluid)	8
Ounces (U.S. fluid)	Gallons (U.S. dry)	0.0067138047
Ounces (U.S. fluid)	Gallons (U.S. liq.)	0.0078125
Ounces (U.S. fluid)	Gills (U.S.)	0.25
Ounces (U.S. fluid)	Liters	0.029572702
Ounces (U.S. fluid)	Pints (U.S. liq.)	0.0625
Ounces (U.S. fluid)	Quarts (U.S. liq.)	0.03125
Ounces/sq. inch	Dynes/sq. cm.	4309.22
Ounces/sq. inch	Grams/sq. cm.	4.3941849
Ounces/sq. inch	Pounds/sq. ft.	9
Ounces/sq. inch	Pounds/sq. inch	0.0625
Parts/million	Grains/gal. (U.S.)	0.05841620
Parts/million	Grams/liter	0.001
Parts/miliion	Milligrams/Liter	1
Pints (U.S. dry)	Bushels (U.S.)	0.015625
Pints (U.S. dry)	Cu. cm.	550.61047
Pints (U.S. dry)	Cu. inches	33.6003125
Pints (U.S. dry)	Gallons (U.S. dry)	0.125
Pints (U.S. dry)	Gallons (U.S. liq.)	0.14545590
Pints (U.S. dry)	Liters	0.5505951
Pints (U.S. dry)	Pecks (U.S.)	0.0625
Pints (U.S. dry)	Quarts (U.S. dry)	0.5
Pints (U.S. liq.)	Cu. cm.	473.17647
Pints (U.S. liq.)	Cu. feet	0.016710069
Pints (U.S. liq.)	Cu. inches	28.875
Pints (U.S. liq.)	Cu. yards	0.00061889146
Pints (U.S. liq.)	Drama (U.S. fluid)	128
Pints (U.S. liq.)	Gallons (U.S. liq.)	0.125
Pints (U.S. liq.)	Gills (U.S.)	4
Pints (U.S. liq.)	Liters	0.4731632

UNITS: CONVERSIONS AND CONSTANTS *(continued)*

FROM	TO	X BY
Pints (U.S. liq.)	Milliliters	473.1632
Pints (U.S. liq.)	Minims (U.S.)	7680
Pints (U.S. liq.)	Ounces (U.S. fluid)	16
Pints (U.S. liq.)	Quarts (U.S. liq.)	0.5
Planck's constant	Erg-seconds	6.6255×10^{-27}
Planck's constant	Joule-seconds	6.6255×10^{-34}
Planck's constant	Joule-sec./Avog. No. (chem.)	3.9905×10^{-10}
Pounds (apoth. or troy)	Drams (apoth. or troy)	96
Pounds (apoth. or troy)	Drams (avdp.)	210.65143
Pounds (apoth. or troy)	Grains	5780
Pounds (apoth. or troy)	Grams	373.24172
Pounds (apoth. or troy)	Kilograms	0.37324172
Pounds (apoth. or troy)	Ounces (apoth. or troy)	12
Pounds (apoth. or troy)	Ounces (avdp.)	13.165714
Pounds (apoth. or troy)	Pounds(avdp.)	0.8228571
Pounds (avdp.)	Drams (apoth. or troy)	116.6686
Pounds (avdp.)	Drams (avdp.)	256
Pounds (avdp.)	Grains	7000
Pounds (avdp.)	Grams	453.59237
Pounds (avdp.)	Kilograms	0.45359237
Pounds (avdp.)	Ounces (apoth. or troy)	14.593333
Pounds (avdp.)	Ounces (avdp.)	16
Pounds (avdp.)	Pounds (apoth. or troy)	1.215277
Pounds (avdp.)	Scruples (apoth.)	350
Pounds (avdp.)	Tons (long)	0.00044642857
Pounds (avdp.)	Tons (metric)	0.00045359237
Pounds (avdp.)	Tons (short)	0.0005
Pounds/cu.ft.	Grams/cu. cm.	0.016018463
Pounds/cu.ft.	Kg./cu. meter	16.018463
Pounds/cu. inch	Grams/cu. cm.	27.679905
Pounds/cu. inch	Grams/liter	27.68068
Pounds/cu. inch	Kg./cu. meter	27679.005
Pounds/gal.(U. S.liq.)	Grams/cu. cm.	0.11982643
Pounds/gal.(U. S.liq.)	Pounds/cu. ft.	7.4805195
Pounds/inch	Grams/cm	178.57967
Pounds/inch	Grams/ft.	5443.1084
Pounds/inch	Grams/inch	453.59237
Pounds/inch	Ounces/cm.	6.2992
Pounds/inch	Ounces/inch	16
Pounds/inch	Pounds/meter	39.370079
Pounds/minute	Kilograms/hr.	27.2155422
Pounds/minute	Kilograms/min.	0.45359237

UNITS: CONVERSIONS AND CONSTANTS *(continued)*

FROM	TO	X BY
Pounds on Earth =1	Pounds on Mars	0.3627 Equatorial
Pounds on Earth =1	Pounds on Mercury	0.3648 Equatorial
Pounds on Earth =1	Pounds on Moon	0.1652 Equatorial
Pounds on Earth =1	Pounds on Neptune	1.323 ± 0.210 Equatorial
Pounds on Earth =1	Pounds on Pluto	0.0225 ± 0.217 Equatorial
Pounds on Earth =1	Pounds on Saturn	0.8800 Equatorial
Pounds on Earth =1	Pounds on Sun	27.905 Equatorial
Pounds on Earth =1	Pounds on Uranus	0.9554 ± 0.168 Equatorial
Pounds on Earth =1	Pounds on Venus	0.9049 Equatorial
Pounds/sq. ft.	Atmospheres	0.000472541
Pounds/sq. ft.	Bars	0.000478803
Pounds/sq. ft.	Cm. of Hg (O°C.)	0.0359131
Pounds/sq. ft.	Dynes/sq. cm.	478.803
Pounds/sq. ft.	Ft. of air (1 atm. 60°F.)	13.096
Pounds/sq. ft.	Grams/sq. cm.	0.48824276
Pounds/sq. ft.	Kg./sq. meter	4.8824276
Pounds/sq. ft.	Mm. of Hg (0°C.)	0.369131
Pounds/sq. inch	Atmospheres	0.0680460
Pounds/sq. inch	Bars	0.0689476
Pounds/sq. inch	Dynes/sq. cm.	68947.6
Pounds/sq. inch	Grams/sq. cm.	70.306958
Pounds/sq. inch	Kg./sq. cm.	0.070306958
Pounds/sq. inch	Mm. of Hg (0°C.)	51.7149
Quarts (U.S. dry)	Bushels (U.S.)	0.03125
Quarts (U.S. dry)	Cu. cm.	1101.2209
Quarts (U.S. dry)	Cu. feet	0.038889251
Quarts (U.S. dry	Cu. inches	67.200625
Quarts (U.S. dry)	Gallons (U.S. dry)	0.25
Quarts (U.S. dry)	Gallons (U.S. liq.)	0.29091180
Quarts (U.S. dry)	Liters	1.1011901
Quarts (U.S. dry)	Pecks (U.S.)	0.125
Quarts (U.S. dry)	Pints (U.S. dry)	2
Quarts (U.S. liq.)	Cu.cm.	946.35295
Quarts (U.S. liq.)	Cu. feet	0.033420136
Quarts (U.S. liq.)	Cu. inches	57.75
Quarts (U.S. liq.)	Drams (U.S. fluid)	256
Quarts (U.S. liq.)	Gallons (U.S. dry)	0.21484175
Quarts (U.S. liq.)	Gallons (U.S. liq.)	0.25
Quarts (U.S. liq.)	Gills (U.S.)	8
Quarts (U.S. liq.)	Liters	0.9463264

UNITS: CONVERSIONS AND CONSTANTS *(continued)*

FROM	TO	X BY
Quarts (U.S. liq.)	Ounces (U.S. fluid)	32
Quarts (U.S. liq.)	Pints (U.S. liq.)	2
Quarts (U.S. liq.)	Quarts (U.S. dry)	0.8593670
Quintals (metric)	Grams	100000
Quintals (metric)	Hundredweights (long)	1.9684131
Quintals (metric)	Kilograms	100
Quintals (metric)	Pounds (avdp.)	220.46226
Radians	Circumferences	0.15915494
Radians	Degrees	57.295779
Radians	Minutes	3437.7468
Radians	Quadrants	0.63661977
Radians	Revolutions	0.15915494
Revolutions	Degrees	360
Revolutions	Grades	400
Revolutions	Quadrants	4
Revolutions	Radians	6.2831853
Seconds (angular)	Degrees	0.000277777
Seconds (angular)	Minutes	0.0166666
Seconds (angular)	Radians	4.8481368×10^{-6}
Seconds (mean solar)	Days (mean solar)	1.1574074×10^{-5}
Seconds (mean solar)	Days (sidereal)	1.1605763×10^{-5}
Seconds (mean solar)	Hours (mean solar)	0.0002777777
Seconds (mean solar)	Hours (sidereal)	0.00027853831
Seconds (mean solar)	Minutes (mean solar)	0.0166666
Seconds (mean solar)	Minutes (sidereal)	0.016712298
Seconds (mean solar)	Seconds (sidereal)	1.00273791
Seconds (sidereal)	Days (mean solar)	1.1542472×10^{-5}
Seconds (sidereal)	Days (sidereal)	1.1574074×10^{-5}
Seconds (sidereal)	Hours (mean solar)	0.00027701932
Seconds (sidereal)	Hours (sidereal)	0.000277777
Seconds (sidereal)	Minutes (mean solar)	0.016621159
Seconds (sidereal)	Minutes (sidereal)	0.0166666
Seconds (sidereal)	Seconds (mean solar)	0.09726957
Sq. Centimeters	Sq. decimeters .	0.01
Sq. centimeters	Sq. feet	0.0010763910
Sq. Centimeters	Sq. inches	0.15500031
Sq. Centimeters	Sq. meters	0.0001
Sq. centimeters	Sq. mm.	100
Sq. centimeters	Sq. mile	155000.31
Sq. centimeters	Sq. yards	0.00011959900
Sq. decimeters	Sq. cm.	100
Sq. Decimeters	Sq. inches	15.500031

UNITS: CONVERSIONS AND CONSTANTS *(continued)*

FROM	TO	X BY
Sq. dekameters	Acres	0.024710538
Sq. dekameters	Ares	1
Sq. dekameters	Sq. meters	100
Sq. dekameters	Sq. yards	119.59900
Sq. feet	Acres	2.295684×10^{-5}
Sq. feet	Ares	0.0009290304
Sq. feet	Sq. cm.	929.0304
Sq. feet	Sq.inches	144
Sq. feet	Sq. meters	0.09290304
Sq. feet	Sq. miles	3.5870064×10^{-8}
Sq. Feet	Sq. yards	0.111111
Sq. Hectometers	Sq. meters	10000
Sq. inches	Sq. cm.	6.4516
Sq. inches	Sq. decimeters	0.064516
Sq. inches	Sq. feet	0.0069444
Sq. inches	Sq. meters	0.00064516
Sq. inches	Sq. miles	$2.4909767 \times 10^{-10}$
Sq. inches	Sq. mm	645.16
Sq. inches	Sq. mils	1×10^{-6}
Sq. kilometers	Acres	247.10538
Sq. Kilometers	Sq. feet	1.0763010×10^{7}
Sq. Kilometers	Sq. inches	1.5500031×10^{9}
Sq. Kilometers	Sq. meters	1×10^{6}
Sq. Kilometers	Sq. miles	0.38610216
Sq. Kilometers	Sq. yards	1.1959900×10^{6}
Sq. meters	Acres	0.00024710538
Sq. meters	Ares	0.01
Sq. meters	Hectares	0.0001
Sq. meters	Sq. cm	10000
Sq. meters	Sq. feet	10.763910
Sq. meters	Sq. inches	1550.0031
Sq. meters	Sq. kilometers	1×10^{-6}
Sq. meters	Sq. miles	3.8610218×10^{-7}
Sq. meters	Sq. mm	1×10^{6}
Sq. meters	Sq. yards	1.1959900
Sq. miles	Acres	640
Sq. miles	Hectares	258.99881
Sq. miles	Sq. feet	2.7878288×10^{7}
Sq. miles	Sq. kilometers	2.5899881
Sq. miles	Sq. meters	2589988.1
Sq. miles	Sq. rods	102400
Sq. miles	Sq. yards	3.0976×10^{6}

UNITS: CONVERSIONS AND CONSTANTS *(continued)*

FROM	TO	X BY
Sq. millimeters	Sq. cm.	0.01
Sq. millimeters	Sq.inches	0.0015500031
Sq. millimeters	Sq. meters	1×10^{-6}
Sq. yards	Acres	0.00020661157
Sq. yards	Ares	0.0083612736
Sq. yards	Hectares	8.3612736×10^{-5}
Sq. yards	Sq. cm	8361.2736
Sq. yards	Sq. feet	9
Sq. yards	Sq. inches	1296
Sq. yards	Sq. meters	0.83612736
Sq. yards	Sq. miles	$3.228305785 \times 10^{-7}$
Tons (long)	Kilograms	1016.0469
Tons (long)	Ounces (avdp.)	35840
Tons (long)	Pounds (apoth. or troy)	2722.22
Tons (long)	Pounds(avdp.)	2240
Tons (long)	Tons (metric)	1.0160469
Tons (long)	Tons (short)	1.12
Tons (metric)	Dynes	9.80665×10^{8}
Tons (metric)	Grams	1×10^{6}
Tons (metric)	Kilograms	1000
Tons (metric)	Ounces (avdp.)	35273.962
Tons (metric)	Pounds (apoth. or troy)	2679.2289
Tons (metric)	Pounde(avdp.)	2204.6226
Tons (metric)	Tons (long)	0.98420653
Tons (metric)	Tons (short)	1.1023113
Tons (short)	Kilograms	907.18474
Tons (short)	Ounces (avdp.)	32000
Tons (short)	Pounds (apoth. or troy)	2430.555
Tons (short)	Pounds(avdp.)	2000
Tons (short)	Tons (long)	0.89285714
Tons (short)	Tons (metric)	0.90718474
Velocity of light	cm/sec. ± 0.33ppm	$2.9979250(10) \times 10^{10}$
Velocity of light	m/sec. ± 0.33ppm	$2.9979250(10) \times 10^{8}$
Velocity of light (100xmore accurate)	Km/sec. ± 1.1 meter/sec.	$2.997924562 \times 10^{5}$
Volts	Mks. (r or nr) units	1
Volts (Int.)	Volts	1.000330
Volt-seconds	Maxwells	1×10^{8}
Watts	Kilowatts	0.001
Watts (Int.)	Watts	1.000165
Weeks (mean calendar)	Days (mean solar)	7
Weeks (mean calendar)	Days (sidereal)	7.0191654
Weeks (mean calendar)	Hours (mean solar)	168

UNITS: CONVERSIONS AND CONSTANTS *(continued)*

FROM	TO	X BY
Weeks (mean calendar)	Hours (sidereal)	168.45997
Weeks (mean calendar)	Minutes (mean solar)	10080
Weeks (mean calendar)	Minutes (sidereal)	10107.598
Weeks (mean calendar)	Months (lunar)	0.23704235
Weeks (mean calendar)	Months (mean calendar)	0.23013699
Weeks (mean calendar)	Years (calendar)	0.019178082
Weeks (mean calendar)	Years (sidereal)	0.019164622
Weeks (mean calendar)	Years (tropical)	0.019165365
Yards	Centimeters	91.44
Yards	Cubits	2
Yards	Fathoms	0.5
Yards	Feet.	3
Yards	Furlongs	0.00454545
Yards	Inches	36
Yards	Meters	0.9144
Yards	Rods	0.181818
Yards	Spans	4
Years (calendar)	Days (mean solar)	365
Years (calendar)	Hours (mean solar)	8760
Years (calendar)	Minutes (mean solar)	525600
Years (calendar)	Months (lunar)	12.360065
Years (calendar)	Months (mean calendar)	12
Years (calendar)	Seconds (mean solar)	3.1536×10^{7}
Years (calendar)	Weeks (mean calendar)	52.142857
Years (calendar)	Years (sidereal)	0.99929814
Years (calendar)	Years (tropical)	0.99933690
Years (leap)	Days (mean solar)	366
Years (sidereal)	Days (mean solar)	365.25636
Years (sidereal)	Days (sidereal)	366.25640
Years (sidereal)	Years (calendar)	1.0007024
Years (sidereal)	Years (tropical)	1.0000388
Years (tropical)	Days (mean solar)	365.24219
Years (tropical)	Days (sidereal)	366.24219
Years (tropical)	Hours (mean solar)	8765.8126
Years (tropical)	Hours (sidereal)	8789.8126
Years (tropical)	Months (mean calendar)	12.007963
Years (tropical)	Seconds (mean solar)	3.1556926×10^{7}
Years (tropical)	Seconds (sidereal)	3.1643326×10^{7}
Years (tropical)	Weeks (mean calendar)	52.177456
Years (tropical)	Years (Calendar)	1.0006635
Years (tropical)	Years (sidereal)	0.99996121

Glossary

A

absolute humidity: the actual amount of water vapor present in the air

alluvial: pertaining to erosion by-products, such as sediment deposited by flowing water

aneroid barometer: an instrument that detects variations in atmospheric pressure by bending a metallic surface, which moves a pointer

aphelion: the point in a planet's orbit that is farthest from the sun

apparent temperature: the actual temperature adjusted for relative humidity; comfort index

aquifer: a water-bearing layer of rock, sand, or gravel

astronomical unit: a unit of length equal to the mean distance of the earth to the sun, or about 93 million miles (150 million kilometers)

atmosphere: thin layer of gases—including nitrogen, oxygen, ozone, and carbon—that surrounds the earth

C

calcite: crystal form of calcium carbonite; component of chalk, limestone, and marble

chemical weathering: the action of airborne acids that damages living and nonliving things near the earth's surface

condensation: the process by which liquid is removed from a vapor

condensation nuclei: a particle of dust, smoke, or other substance that forms the center of a drop of water

conduction: transmission of electricity or heat through a medium

convection: heat transfer resulting from the movement of warmer substances upwards

coquina: soft limestone formed of broken shells and corals

crust: the rocky outer surface of the earth

crystals: the shapes into which nonliving substances, such as salt and ice, grow

D

dew point: the temperature at which air becomes saturated and produces dew

diffraction: the spreading out of waves, such as light waves, as they pass by the edge of an obstacle or through an opening

diffraction grating: a glass plate with parallel grooves or slits; produces optical spectra when white light strikes it

E

escape velocity: the minimum velocity that a body must attain to escape from the gravitational field of the earth or other body

evaporation: the changing of liquid into vapor

erosion: the wearing away of soil and rock caused by the action of air, water, and temperature changes

F

feldspar: mineral occuring in igneous and other rocks; one of the hardest minerals

fossil: imprint or remains of a plant or animal from a past geological age

fossil fuel: fuel, such as coal, that is derived from fossils

G

gravity: the attraction between all objects because of their mass; the force that holds the universe together

H

halite: salt, or sodium chloride, in the form of solid masses; rock salt

hygrometer: an instrument that measures humidity in the air

I

igneous rock: rock formed by the cooling of melted material

inertia: the tendency of a motionless object to remain motionless, or of a moving object to continue moving unless disturbed by an outside force

infrared rays: rays lying slightly beyond the red end of the visible light spectrum; heat rays

inner core: the ball-shaped center of the earth, probably consisting of iron and nickel

isostasy: equilibrium resulting from equal pressure from all directions

L

leeward: located in or facing the direction toward which the wind is blowing

light-year: the distance that light travels in a vacuum in one year—approximately 5,878 trillion miles

lodestone: a magnetized piece of the mineral form of black iron oxide

M

magnitude: the relative brightness of a celestial body indicated on a numerical scale

mantle: thick layer of solid rock between the earth's crust and outer core

mirror telescope: telescope that uses a mirror rather than a lens to gather light; reflecting telescope

MOHS hardness scale: scale that lists ten minerals from softest to hardest. The hardness of other minerals can be determined by scratching them with minerals on the scale.

moraine: stones and debris carried along and deposited by a glacier; a ridge of debris on the surface of or at the edge of a glacier

O

outer core: thick layer of melted iron and nickel between the earth's mantle and inner core

P

parallax: apparent change in the position of an object, caused by a change in position from which the object is viewed

penumbra: a partial shadow between a perfect shadow and full light

perihelion: the point nearest the sun in a planet's orbit

photochemical: relating to the interactions of radiant energy and chemical systems

prism: a wedge-shaped transparent object used to disperse a beam of light, producing a spectrum

psychrometer: a type of hygrometer that uses the difference between the reading of two thermometers to measure humidity

R

radiation: the emission of radiant energy in the form of waves or particles

radio astronomy: the study of celestial objects by analyzing radio-frequency waves received from outside the earth's atmosphere

radiometer: an instrument that detects and measures radiation

refracting telescope: telescope that produces an enlarged image through the use of lenses

relative humidity: the amount of water vapor in the air compared to the maximum amount possible

revolution: the orbital motion of planets around the sun

rhyolite: glassy volcanic rock; the lava form of granite

rotation: the motion of earth and other planets on their axes

S

saturation: the point at which air at a specific temperature or soil is unable to hold more moisture; 100% relative humidity

sediment: material that settles to the bottom of a liquid

sedimentary rock: rock formed from sediment or from fragments transported by water

specific heat capacity: the amount of heat required to raise the temperature of a body one degree

spectroscopy: the study of spectra; using a spectroscope

spectrum: a band of colors produced when light passes through a prism and spreads out. Different light sources produce different spectra.

stalactite: rock formation hanging down from the roof of a cave, formed by the dripping of calcite-rich water

stalagmite: rock formation projecting upwards from the floor of a cave, formed by the dripping of calcite-rich water

streaking: scratching a mineral on a hard white surface to examine the color of the powder as a means of identification

T

tectonic plates: moving plates composing the earth's crust and upper mantle. The motion of the plates past each other is believed to cause most earthquakes, mountains, and volcanoes.

thermal inversion: condition that occurs when a layer of stationary warm air settles over a layer of cool air, causing pollution near the ground

thermocline: a layer that separates an upper, warmer zone of water from a lower, colder heavier zone

transpiration: the process of giving off watery vapor through animal or plant pores

trough: depression or lowest point between ocean waves

U

ultraviolet rays: rays located beyond the visible spectrum at its violet end

umbra: the darkest part of a shadow; part of a shadow from which all light is excluded

W

weathering: physical and chemical processes by which weather decomposes earth materials

windward: located in or facing the direction from which the wind blows

Index